*In the
Tiger's Mouth*

KATRINA SHIELDS

In the Tiger's Mouth

AN EMPOWERMENT
GUIDE FOR
SOCIAL ACTION

Cartoons by Phil Somerville

NEW SOCIETY PUBLISHERS
Philadelphia, PA   *Gabriola Island, BC*

Originally published in Australia by Millenium Books, an imprint of E.J. Dwyer
Pty. Ltd. in 1991.

Inquiries regarding requests to reprint all or part of *In the Tiger's Mouth: An
Empowerment Guide for Social Action* should be addressed to New Society
Publishers, 4527 Springfield Avenue, Philadelphia, PA, 19143.

ISBN Hardcover   USA 0-86571-286-7   CAN 1-55092-232-7
ISBN Paperback   USA 0-86571-287-5   CAN 1-55092-233-5

Cover design by Toni Hope-Caten. Text design by Norman Baptista. Typeset in
11/13 Bembo by Post Typesetters of Queensland, Australia. Printed in the United
States of America on partially recycled paper using soy ink by Capital City Press of
Montpelier, Vermont.

® GCIU ™-c

To order directly from the publisher, add $2.50 to the price for the first copy, 75¢
each additional. Send check or money order to:

In the United States: *In Canada:*
New Society Publishers   New Society Publishers/New Catalyst
4527 Springfield Avenue   PO Box 189
Philadelphia, PA 19143   Gabriola Island, BC VOR 1XO

New Society Publishers is a project of the New Society Educational Foundation, a
nonprofit, tax-exempt, public foundation in the United States, and of the Catalyst
Education Society, a nonprofit society in Canada. Opinions expressed in this book
do not necessarily represent positions of the New Society Educational Foundation,
nor the Catalyst Education Society.

About the author

‑‑‑

As part of a Consultancy Team, Katrina Shields leads workshops, provides training, renewal retreats and empowerment counselling for non-profit community groups and government agencies throughout Australia.

Her experiences as an activist on community development, environment, women's and peace issues inspired her to explore more effective and sustainable means.

Katrina is a facilitator for the Interhelp Network and is currently involved in establishing a Heart Politics Conference and Retreat Centre near her home base — Lismore, in Northern New South Wales.

She loves doing playback theatre, clowning, dancing and sitting on the verandah listening to frogs.

Any reader interested in organising or attending workshops or Training sessions may contact P.O. Box 416, Lismore, NSW, 2480, Australia.

Dedication

••

This book is dedicated to those many unsung heroes and heroines who have worked for peace, justice and ecological sanity; and to those who are yet to emerge.

Contents

Acknowledgments

As I bring to mind all the people to whom I would like to express my appreciation, for supporting me and helping shape this book, the list keeps growing. This is because this work grew out of the context of a caring, active and supportive community that spans several networks.

One who springs to mind immediately is James Bennett-Levy — without whose help in many forms and his belief in me and the project — the book would never have been completed. Many others have also been very generous in their practical, financial or moral support such as Nan and Hugh Nicolson, the late Francis Wigham, Joanna Macy, Nadine Hood, Pat Fleming, Pedro McDade, Anthea Duquemin, Cathy Picone, Kath Fisher, Bobbi and John Allen, Annie Kia, Fran Peavey, Tova Green, Simon Clough (and his Aunt Peggy), Patrick Anderson, Gai Longmuir, Stu Anderson, Ken Golding, Annie Bolitho, Laurie Jamieson, Brian Slapp, Friedmann Weiland, Christopher Titmuss, Max Lawson, Steve Gunther, Bruce Semler, Shirley Sabravo, Shepherd Bliss, Pam Gray, Kerith Power, Jill Trevillian, Denice Nagorka and those other wonderful women in my women's group. I would like to thank my mother Brenda Shields, my sister Bronwyn Shields, my aunt Pat Lindsay and brother Terry Beck for their tangible help and support.

A special group of computer whizzes deserve a big thankyou! Jane Miknius and my late friend John Carter for access to computers; also trouble shooting and key-boarding at various points from Stephen Hodgkins, David Mantle, Bill Kidd and Margaret Reid.

People who were sources of inspiration, influence on my work and gave valuable information — though some of them do not know it: Joanna Macy, Hugh Crago, Ann Herbert, Kevin McVeigh, Fran Peavey, Bridgit Brandon, Richard Moss and Bill Moyer — to name a few.

To all these and others I am grateful. Finally I would like to thank the many leaders whose workshops I drew material from, and my clients and workshop participants who also contributed much.

The author gratefully acknowledges the use of material from the following works. Every effort has been made to locate the sources of quoted material and to obtain authorization for its use.

Heart Politics, Fran Peavey, New Society Publishers: Philadelphia, PA, Santa Cruz, CA, and Gabriola Island, BC; 800–333–9093.

How Can I Help? by Ram Dass and Paul Gorman, copyright © by Ram Dass and Paul Gorman, reprinted by permission of Alfred A. Knopf.

"Preventing Burnout in the Public Interest Community," Dr. William L. Bryan, NRAG Papers, Vol. 3, No. 3, Northern Rockies Action Group, Helena, Montana, USA.

The Tao of Leadership, John Heider, © 1985, Humanics Publishing Group, Atlanta, Georgia.

Preface by Joanna Macy

There are many recipes for the Good Life, ranging from ancient spiritual practices to the latest techniques for health, wealth and self-improvement. In whatever various ways we may define it, after all that is what we want — a Good Life.

What is striking to me in today's world is the growing number of people for whom the Good Life involves some form of social change work. I find more and more people of all ages and walks of life wanting to make a difference in their world. They see the social and economic injustices, the dangers of nuclear disaster and environmental destruction— and instead of burying their heads in the sand and going on with business-as-usual, they want to take part in the healing of their world.

This in itself is wonderfully promising; yet the sad fact is that only a small portion of those who want this manage to make social action a sustained and sustaining part of their lives. Many are stopped before they start — stopped by feelings of isolation, by notions that they don't possess the necessary expertise or moral stamina, or by fears of losing control of their lives. Others who do take the plunge and engage in activist campaigns, eventually burn out, withdraw in fatigue — as is evident from the high turnover in many change organizations. For all of these, be they the self-distrusting or the battle-weary, it is not enough to keep sounding the alarm of planetary peril, or by repeating exhortations to social responsibility.

For these many — and indeed for us all — we need a recipe book that connects the personal with the political, the inner with the outer. We need a compilation of easy, practical methods for embarking on social action, and sustaining and enjoying it, so that it is no longer seen as a daunting, demanding exercise in self-sacrifice. We need pointers for finding our own deep sources of energy and vision, so that our work for the world runs like an ever-refreshing stream through our lives.

Here, praise be, is such a recipe book. This volume offers in an inviting, accessible form just the kind of help we all need for finding personal fulfillment and effectiveness in social change work.

I am delighted that it is offered to us by so wise and compassionate a woman as Katrina Shields. As a trained occupational therapist, a gifted counsellor, a veteran activist and group empowerment facilitator, she has a rich storehouse of skills and experience on which to draw. And she shares it generously, with a kind of luminous humility. I love it that this book is so free of cant, so deceptively simple in tone, so perceptive and respectful of our humanity.

Whether you are an old hand in social change work or new to the game, there is rich fare for you in these pages. In addition to the author's own reflections and experience, we find stories from the lives of many activists, and an array of personal and group exercises so appealing and practical that one itches to try them straight off. Reading them I am reminded once again that the greatest challenge of our time can also be our greatest joy — to join together in the healing of our world.

Joanna Macy PhD

Introduction

--◆--

Some twelve years ago I was living a relatively isolated life in a rural community in the semitropical rainforest of northern New South Wales. We were growing food, building and devoting time to meditation practice. A gentle Buddhist monk from Thailand had temporarily joined our group of 20 adults and 15 children, to seek refuge from political harassment for organizing controversial social justice activities in his home country. He came one day and silently left a beautiful rice paper brush and ink drawing on the floor of our simple abode in the forest. It was of a rampant tiger with the caption "The best place for meditation is in the tiger's mouth".

It proved prophetic in a way, as soon we came to be embroiled in struggles to save the remnant rainforests nearby and many of us were awakened to the vastly wider context of the issue. There were many other issues that I, along with this group and others, have been involved in since, spanning community development, social empowerment, welfare, peace, women's and environmental issues.

I lead a very different life now and so does the monk. I still have the painting on my wall. The ongoing enquiry for me is how to maintain an open heart and open mind, while in the tiger's mouth.

It is a useful metaphor for the danger and opportunity inherent in our situation. Whether we acknowledge it or not, we are, collectively, in the tiger's mouth in a way which transcends all national boundaries. We are at risk of being overwhelmed by our wastes, of undermining our life support systems, and being damaged by our own technology — not to mention creating staggering inequalities between peoples of the world. The list could continue...

The opportunity is that through all this we are forced to recognize our interconnectedness with the earth, other species and each other as a reality, and base our actions on that knowledge. We could find truly sustainable means of production and consumption that take the future into account. Social justice issues need to be addressed. We will be challenged to find ways to empower individuals, communities and nations to discover cooperative solutions. Doing this will require us to really work together in ways we perhaps only get glimpses of now.

The metaphor also applies individually: to the danger and opportunity inherent in being aware and involved in social change work; the danger of literally being paralyzed by the enormity of the problems, or crushed or consumed by the jaws of our over-involvement. There is also the danger of staying stuck in a victim role, or of maintaining an oppositional or enemy mentality. Another danger is thinking there is only one solution (and *we* already have it!).

The situation also requires us to act within ourselves, inside our own lives. Our personal challenge is to clear away the habits of exploitation, oppression and submission. We may also find out: What part of us is in the tiger? And how are we feeding it?

We need to attend to these inner changes hand in hand with our outer action. Fortunately this inner work acts in tandem with our outer actions by providing the motivation and inner resources to sustain our quality of action.

In the last few years in Australia I have observed a big increase in disillusionment and cynicism with current political structures. No doubt this is also true in other places. It is dawning on more and more people that it won't be governments who will lead us to solve the enormous problems that we face. Hopefully governments will, at best, follow. It will be up to individuals who have a sense of empowerment, local communities and grass-roots groups to take the initiative. Change will also come from caring and brave individuals "within the systems" who take a stand.

There have been many inspiring examples of this work, such as the citizen diplomacy movement between citizens of the USA and the USSR. In that case many ordinary people did not wait for officials to drop their national paranoia, but reached out and met the real people behind the labels and rhetoric.

This book is based on several assumptions. The first is that we humans, much of the time, are not especially rational beings. We have a lot of information about the danger we are in, and I do believe that most of us care about what that means. Yet many of us do not respond, or we respond in token ways to assuage our guilt. Our capacity for denial, and widespread feelings of fear and powerlessness cannot be ignored or solved with just more information on the dangers. This book explores what else we need.

For those who can and do respond, the effectiveness of a disturbing amount of their action is jeopardized by poor relationships, disillusionment, isolation and exhaustion in the long run. It can be a great struggle to integrate political work into personal lives. This book is about applying practical tools to solve these dilemmas.

It also assumes that the means need to be consistent with the ends we seek, if the achievement of goals is to have lasting benefits. This means adherence to nonviolence, not only the absence of violence, but also a positive commitment to building relationships and communities. By employing these means we can learn to reach out across gulfs to resolve conflict and find ways to appreciate and integrate diversity rather than shun it. We can learn to expand from within while still taking a firm stand on and refusing to cooperate with destruction and oppression. There cannot be just one way to solve the myriad problems, nor one ideology or lifestyle that can unite us.

This book also assumes that each of us has a unique contribution to make to the world in responding to the call of this time. When we give what we have to offer fully, this can be a replenishing and enriching process, a path with a heart. I assume we do not have to settle for less. I also assume that if we nurture and support our own and each other's capacities, this sum total could bring the needed solutions and changes. I know we are capable of much more than we are seeing at present — and there was never a riper, more pressing time for this flowering to take place.

So who is this book for? Whether your concerns focus on the environment, peace issues, social justice, women's, youth, community development or welfare issues, the same principles apply, and the exercises are appropriate for all these different contexts.

Are you somebody who has some concerns, yet feels powerless to translate them into action?

Or are you someone who has made some forays into the arena of organizing social change — perhaps by joining a group or a campaign or working for a public interest organization — but find yourself disillusioned with the process or people's attitudes, and are tempted to or have actually withdrawn?

Or perhaps you have long experience of working for change, yet feel battle-weary and wonder if there is a way of sustainable activism that doesn't cost you your vitality, relationships and your ideals.

If you can identify with these scenarios this book provides some pointers to finding different ways and means.

One of the many challenges in writing a book such as this is to find a language that is not alienating. This is one of the central problems in social activism and stops us identifying with each other as allies. Words and labels such as "activist", "greeny", "feminist", "concerned citizen" or even "political organizer" can have loaded connotations and conjure up images that we wish to avoid being stereotyped with: "Well no, I'm not one of *those*." We don't see the commonality of concerns — that we might be working for similar changes. (For instance is the opposite of activist a pacifist? — obviously it is possible to be both!) As a reader, feel free to blot out the ones you don't like and insert ones you can relate to.

Another sensitive area is referring to spirituality in the social change context. Remember the exhortation never to mix religion and politics? At first I thought the best thing would be to avoid mentioning it altogether, to play it safe, as it is too easy to be misunderstood on this subject and I feel some awkwardness about handling it.

I, like many, am grappling with the meaning of spirituality and have in the past been very put off by the rigidity and oppression which has occurred in the name of some organized religions over the centuries. Yet a spiritual perspective is implicit in much that I have said. And I believe also that many movements have benefited from breaking the taboo by talking more openly about our spiritual sources. The schism between spirituality and politics needs to be healed.

The book is divided into three sections:
The first section concentrates on the personal inner obstacles that we may face in becoming involved with changing the status quo, and developing the inner resources to respond and to stay involved. There are chapters dealing with difficult feelings, believing you can make a difference, building a support base, nurturing vision and cultivating insight into your own projections and the consequences of these.

The second section focusses on practical tools for effectiveness in outer action. This encompasses chapters on bridge building with the opposition,

effective listening as a social change tool, giving talks on bad news with a view to empowerment, working together cooperatively, new leadership paradigms and forming support groups.

The third section looks specifically at the issue of burnout — both the contribution that individual habits and motivations make to whether you end up burning out or not, and the way organizations, despite the best of intentions, end up burning out workers. Also I include a section on how to renew oneself after an experience of burnout.

There are throughout the book *exercises* to stimulate further exploration of the content. Some only take a few minutes; a few could take at least an hour. The majority of the exercises have been designed to be done either alone or in groups. They could form the basis of workshops or be useful in gatherings. If you intend to use them in workshops please first read Chapter 14 which gives suggestions on how to facilitate and structure them. Some of these exercises can potentially evoke strong feelings which need to be handled responsibly by a group leader.

Checklists and rating scales are also spread throughout the text to stimulate reflection.

As this book is concerned with solving serious social issues, my treatment can slide towards earnestness. This is not my intention. After all, having fun, delighting in each other and enjoying our roles as we heal ourselves and our world is the most subversive and enduring path to change. Is it not our aim to build social change movements that are attractive — which therefore effortlessly attract others to join in and make their own contribution? It need not be a grim, selfless struggle, relying on moral pressure and blackmail to make us do our bit.

Please read between the lines encouragement to find humor in the absurdity of it all, to enjoy life, to love each other and rest deeply.

Inner Resources for Social Change

CHAPTER ONE

The Dilemmas of Awakening

The sun is shining as I walk outside into the delightful garden. I feel the freshness, and drink in the beauty of the lush sub-tropical vegetation. The birds are warbling, crickets and cicadas are in full cry. Then a wave of unease passes through me: "Maybe it is not safe to be in the sun". I have been hearing things about the ozone layer damage, the high risk of skin cancer, the weakening of the immune system. I was sick for a long time. Had I already been affected? I push that thought aside. How could it possibly be true? . . . ah the garden, this lovely morning.

Sitting on the veranda, my musing turns to thoughts of my work, of where I want to take my career. Any projections beyond 12 months run into a big BUT: "BUT what is happening to our world?" Our planet is in trouble. What about my life? But there is work to be done to sort out this mess. . . The enormity of the prospective problems passes like a cloud across the sun. It makes the idea of planning for the longer term rather meaningless . . . I want to enjoy this day, now . . .

I wander along the country road through the village. I see between the lantana bushes and the tall ragweed the glint of the trash : cans and plastic bags. How is this possible? How can people do that! I feel angry and sad. Wandering on, I enjoy the shimmer of the sun reflecting off the river . . . nice day for a swim. But the water isn't really clean enough here — remember the sewage, the herbicides and other sprays upstream.

Yet I know I am living in one of the more beautiful and unspoilt parts of the lucky country — Australia. Images come to mind of what is happening to brothers and sisters around the world. My friend works with refugees — many of whom are victims of torture; he hears stories that are beyond belief . . . El Salvador, Afghanistan, South Africa.

Closer to home I remember the stories told by my counselling clients — battered wives, terrified children. What we are capable of doing to each other! The nuclear cloud has not dispersed yet; more countries have joined the nuclear club . . .

I wander on, trying to bring my mind back to the present, to savor

"The psychology of the individual is reflected in the psychology of the nation . . . Only a change in attitude of the individual can initiate a change in the psychology of the nation." Carl Jung.

this moment... but the feelings linger on. All is not well... What is going to become of us?

Often I think our society is at an adolescent stage developmentally. We're too busy burning round in fast cars to notice where we are. We're fascinated by bright new playthings —focussed on "Me first." Puffed up bullies saunter along the beach threatening to kick sand in our faces. Who cares about the future? We consume to fill the emptiness inside and try to prove we're OK. We don't really notice the junk we leave behind or who is paying for it. Nor do we notice all the kids who get left out of the party. Perhaps, underneath, there are hopes and dreams, idealism and caring, but we're too afraid of showing it lest we get teased, lest we stand out from the mediocre bunch.

THE NATURE OF CRISIS

In this section I will share some inner obstacles I have met in myself and others — obstacles to finding sane and constructive responses to living with this madness. These responses require strengthening inner resources for moving into action. The times in which we live are very uncertain, often frightening and yet exciting. How can one stay open, caring and responsive in the face of the threats and still live a healthy and sustainable life?

I know I am among the fortunate minority who even have the luxury of the dilemma. For many the holocaust has already started. I'm not preoccupied with immediate survival, I don't have to feed a starving family. I'm not confronted with crippling oppression and turmoil so that getting through each day is a victory in itself. We are the fortunate minority who are best placed to initiate many of the solutions. We are also living the western lifestyle which has created the problems.

Ours is the first generation faced with this daunting task. As Jonathan Schell puts it "Each of us is called on to do something that no member of any generation before ours has had to do: to assume responsibility for the continuation of our kind — to choose human survival... For the risk of extinction is not just one more item on the agenda of issues that face us. Embracing as it does, the life and death of every human being on earth and every future human being, it embraces and transcends all other issues."[1] Yet collectively we are only just starting to acknowledge that the problem exists. When will we cross the threshold to say "Enough! — This is my responsibility"?

We have been given warnings that we have little time — five, maybe ten years — to turn this around or "we face, by the end of the century, an environmental catastrophe as complete, as irreversible as any nuclear holocaust," says Dr Mustafe Tolba, Director-General of the United Nations Environment Program.

Like any crisis, the potential for change — for better or worse — is thrown wide open! It may just keep getting worse. We may make some token gestures, some superficial reforms, then join the ones for whom the holocaust has already arrived. Alternatively the danger will suddenly awaken deep life-preserving instincts in each of us, which catalyze strengths, resources and innovations we did not previously realize we had.

Whether we can respond or not, has a lot to do with how we handle our feelings; because, as Fran Peavey, author of *Heart Politics* says: "One's feet move most determinedly when one's head and heart are both engaged."

Consider the possibility of global catastrophe occurring in our lifetime. What feelings do you get?

The Kinds of Feelings I've Had:

I don't want to know that...

I didn't hear that, turn up the stereo, please not now...

Denial is sometimes useful — it helps us to not get overwhelmed, not to bite off more than we can chew. But it also stops us hearing the information that there is a problem. When we are in denial we want others to be in it too.

Yeah, but what has that got to do with me?

I've got enough on my plate...

Maybe I will be OK, maybe it will get bad somewhere else.

I don't care!

As if I didn't belong, as if I were an island! Aren't I lucky — getting one of the good deck chairs on the Titanic!

It's just too big, what is the point of feeling anything?

I can't afford to care.

I might burst if I felt the pain...

How could "They" do anything that will really help?

You can't change the system — it's run by important men.

How could I really make a difference? ... (Besides, I'm busy)

Where would I start?

I might have to do it on my own.

If I sound interested, they might make me join something.

I'm furious that I can't just enjoy my life. Why can't the world be a safe place? ... How dare they!

I thought I could trust them.. I thought they knew what they were doing.

I'm scared for my children. I am just so scared of what might happen.

If I tell people what I feel, they will think I'm really neurotic.

What's wrong with being emotional! It's the death of my future!

Panic! I've got to DO something, anything, now: make all those idiots see! There is not enough time!

I have had all these reactions at different times. Are any familiar to you?

"DESPAIR WORK" AND TRUST

Some fortunate encounters have had a profound effect on me in transforming these feelings. The first was reading Joanna Macy's book, *Despair and Personal Power in the Nuclear Age*[2]. I drank it in! Here was somebody saying that my feelings were a sane reaction to an insane situation. It was important and useful to let myself feel them fully — they would not break me. (In fact, numbness was hard work!) They were important because they held the key to my energy and motivation to act.

What a relief! I was not just neurotic to care so strongly about what was happening to my world. This led to a rich and fruitful journey with people from many parts of the world. I participated in and led gatherings, workshops and support groups, as part of a loose network called Interhelp. We grieved together, we raged at injustice — using processes called *despairwork* — and came to celebrate the transformative potential inherent in the essence of life. We taught each other skills for being more effective change agents, we participated in actions, we challenged each other to extend further and to express the truth of what we saw was happening in our world in places where the taboos were strong. We also had a lot of fun together.

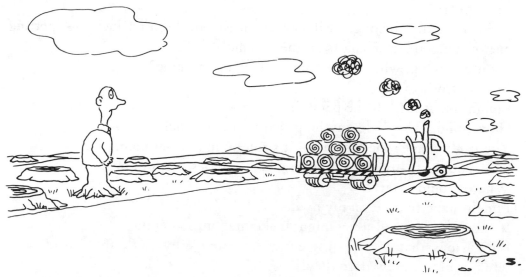

For many of us this process uncovered a trust in our personal power. Moreover, new energy and creativity that had been occluded by trying to numb out those feelings was released. Activists who were exhausted from the fray had a chance to revitalize. Many found a way to begin.

Initially we focussed on the nuclear threat — that was what loomed largest then. We also met in women's groups to explore the implications of living in a violent, male-dominated world. The men gathered to explore new dimensions of being that had been denied them by restrictive conditioning. Other times we gathered in the forests to deepen our understanding of our bonds with the earth and other species. More recently we have focussed on what it means in each of our lives to engage in "Heart Politics".

Our culture has so many ways to discourage us from knowing what we really feel and who we really are: the "tranquilization by the trivial", the endless distraction, busyness, pressure to have and be more and more. Yet there is so much information around now that says "WE are in DANGER". Me. You. Our children. The sky, the water, and lots of our fellow creatures.

We need a bridge between information and action. Just scaring each other with more and more graphic and terrifying bad news won't necessarily activate us. I believe that bridge is created by honoring our feelings, our deep knowing and caring; and being prepared to face the vulnerability that comes from that. We may also need assistance to identify our strengths and what we can uniquely offer. We also need support, to hold each other accountable to continue taking steps that will best express our truth, as we help each other to uncover it. It is from taking action that the fear and powerlessness begin to transform themselves.

We do not need to do this alone; nor does it need to be in fancy workshops, with slick leaders, in special places.

There are people everywhere who care deeply about what is happening to our world. Apparent apathy is so often just a cover. If they are given an opportunity to be heard, many are willing to express their concerns and move into constructive action. Through admitting that we do care deeply about these things we can discover a fuller sense of belonging to all of life and begin to feel our power to act on its behalf. I believe that from this source anything is possible.

EXERCISES

For me, reading Rachael Carson's *Silent Spring* when I was in high school was a profound turning point in the way I perceived my world. It brought home to me, graphically, how widespread were the threats to the environment and how they were interrelated. It also changed my view of "the experts". What I found was how often they were involved in suppressing or playing down information that was in fact vital to our survival.

Sharing stories in this way can be a powerful yet simple way of validating

Telling our waking up stories

the commonality of our concerns about things we often don't talk about. It also helps us to find or reconfirm commitment.

Sit silently for a minute to remember significant moments when you first became aware of some aspect of the planetary crisis.

● **What event changed your perception of the way things are?**

● **What were you thinking and feeling at the time?**

If you are doing this exercise in a group, take 3–10 minutes per person to listen without interruption or discussion as each person tells his/her story. If anyone in the group shows strong feelings, it is important for the group leader to validate those reactions. Don't try to cheer people up; to listen supportively is all that is needed. It is good to follow up this kind of exercise with one of an empowering nature.

Recognizing our "double lives"

There are many times when I recognize the lack of congruence between what I know needs changing and the so-called "pragmatic choices" I make to fit in with "life as usual". One instance is driving my car, yet knowing the impact of this on the environment. Another is thinking about career choices aimed at a good wage and future prospects versus the knowledge of a world in crisis.

The purpose of this exercise is to bring into focus the tension of the incongruity. Living more ecologically accrues from many changes to our lifestyle. It is important to recognize that we are in times of transition, and where we'd like to be and where we are is far apart. Congratulate yourself for being willing to question things that have been taken for granted. Self-flagellation is a waste of time. So if this exercise is done in a group setting, it is important to avoid the group becoming moralistic or self-righteous.

Divide into pairs or threes. Take up to 5 minutes each to speak about your conflicts between what you know and how you live.

● **When in your life are you most aware of inner conflict or of living a double life? How do you feel about this?**

There are not necessarily instant solutions to these dilemmas. However, you could follow this with a discussion on what action you are able to take to bring your behavior more in line with your convictions.

● **How else can your needs be met? Which needs are more important**

in the overall scheme of things? Whose cooperation is needed in making these changes?

We find so many ways and reasons to hold back and stay silent even about things we do care deeply about. The purpose of this exercise is to clarify and give impetus to speaking out about issues of concern, whether they be about the environment, social justice or neighborhood issues. It can be done alone or in pairs.

Speaking out about our concerns

If in pairs take it in turns to finish the following open sentences. Partner A asks B to complete all of these sentences, then swaps over. Don't interrupt or comment while your partner is answering. Take a maximum of 2 minutes for each question.
1. **The things I feel really concerned about are . . .**
2. **If I were feeling strong and powerful, what I'd like to speak out about is..**
3. **The person or people I'd really like to address this to is/are . . .**
4. **The things that will help me speak up are . . .**
5. **The circumstances that would assist my concerns being listened to are . . .**
6. **The ways I avoid or stop myself from doing this are . . .**
7. **My worst fantasy about what might happen if I spoke up is . . .**
8. **What I am willing to do about speaking up in the next week is . . .**

The purpose of this exercise is to pinpoint at which level we (or others) may be denying reality — which in turn prevents problem-solving and changes of behavior. It introduces a model which can be applied to a personal problem such as smoking or getting on with your parents; equally it can apply to issues of social concern such as pollution or social injustice.[3]

The hierarchy of denial

DENIAL OF:	
Personal ability to act on solutions	Level 6–Personal ability
Personal ability to choose viable solutions	Level 5–Personal ability
Solvability of problem Possibility of change	Level 4–Change
Existence or viability of options	Level 3–Options
Existence or significance of problems	Level 2–Problems
Existence of information	Level 1–Information

According to this model we will deny or discount all those levels above the one on which we are blocked.

For instance, take the paper mill pollution issue in Australia to illustrate the different levels of denial. Some of the paper companies tried to deny that these mills did expel dioxins in the waste water and suppressed information that would establish this (Level 1). Others in power have played down the significance of dioxins entering the rivers and ocean; yet dioxins are highly toxic pollutants (Level 2).

The argument that there are no other viable options, if we want paper and jobs, was also put forward (Level 3). When these arguments were proved false the next level of objections was: these options cannot be implemented or the consumers will not accept unbleached paper products (Level 4). Then, towards the apex of the pyramid, are people who are concerned but feel unable to influence events because they are denying their power as consumers and /or activists (Level 5). On the last step in denial are those who recognize they could make a difference but doubt their ability to implement it (Level 6).

SECTION A

Choose a particular issue of concern for you.

Use these questions to bring into focus at what level the denial is operating.

1st level: To what extent is the information about the problem being suppressed or denied?

2nd level: To what extent is the fact that it is a problem (or its seriousness) being played down? For instance, by saying "There are more important issues"... "We haven't got time..."

3rd level: To what extent are you/others saying "We do have a problem, but we'll just have to live with it. Nothing can be done"?

4th level: To what extent are you/others saying things like "There might be other ways of doing it but the obstacles are just too big... or it will cost too much... take too long... what can one person do?"

5th level: To what extent are you/others denying your personal ability to think through the situation? Is there doubt that you can make a difference or choose a workable direction? Do you/they believe there is no support?

6th level: To what extent are you/ others denying your ability to act differently and follow through the chosen direction?

SECTION B–Problem solving
Having established where you are on the denial hierarchy, the following questions will help you move towards a solution.

Questions to ask yourself on a personal issue.
   Where are you stuck with this issue?
   What does this imply?
   What do you need in order to shift?
   Where do you feel most capable of acting on this issue?

Applying the model on a social issue:
   What are the main levels of denial?
   Are people you are targeting at different levels of denial?

   At what level is your campaign information or action aimed? Is this appropriate?
   Having identified the level where particular groups or individuals are blocked, what is the appropriate strategy to shift that denial?

NOTES
1. Jonathan Schell, "The Abolition, Defining The Great Predicament", *New Yorker Magazine*, January, 1984.

2. Joanna Macy, *Despair and Personal Power in the Nuclear Age*, New Society Publishers, Philadelphia, 1983.

3. The hierarchy of denial model I present here is a simplified and adapted version from Transactional Analysis theory (based on the work of Ken Mellor and Eric Schiff).

CHAPTER TWO

Making a Difference

"It is individuals who change societies, who give birth to ideas, who by standing out against the tides of opinion, change them." — Doris Lessing.

"Nobody makes a greater mistake than he who did nothing because he could do only a little." — Edmund Burke, 18th century statesman.

I heard a story recently of a young Irish woman, less than twenty, with no political background, who worked at the check-out counter in a large supermarket in Dublin. She was aware of the apartheid regime in South Africa, and the fact that the black people there had called on consumers not to buy South African products. Because her store carried South African fruit she decided to refuse to sell it. At work she rang up all the other goods but not the products from South Africa. Customers complained, managers came. She was fired. By the end of the day all the women in the store were refusing to sell South African fruit.

The strife escalated, with threats of mass stand-downs and workers in other supermarkets coming out in support of the women who refused to sell the racist fruit. The issue was covered in the press and on television and many people in Ireland learnt about the real cost of cheap apartheid fruit. Eventually the company agreed to stop selling South African fruit, the young woman got her job back and in the process, the whole community had learnt about the power of one person's commitment to act in solidarity with those who are oppressed.

The essential changes will require a lot of individuals taking action on many levels; but to do so requires a belief that you as an individual, and the individuals around you, can make a difference. We see from this example that "people power" grows from a base of individual empowerment.

We may have to face this obstacle of powerlessness, in many guises, over and over again. We may say "But what can I do? I haven't got what it takes." "I am not a real... (activist, environmentalist, political person, feminist, peace worker etc.)" As Kevin McVeigh, the former US Interhelp Coordinator, points out: "The denial of power is as endemic to our culture as the denial of feelings."

It is the idea of powerlessness which is the obstacle, rather than actual powerlessness. When we find ways to disperse or overcome this belief in powerlessness, coupled with motivation from a clear perception of the danger we are in, we can act in creative and life-enhancing ways. We generally don't need to be told what to do — we tend to figure it out quite quickly, guided by our inner sense, if we are willing to listen to it.

Developing this sense of empowerment is to discover our capacity to bring about outer, and inner, change. Inner change entails purposefully transforming our habitual responses to life. It also implies accepting personal responsibility. Acting on our own and others' behalf, we may protest and refuse to cooperate with things we know to be detrimental; or we may investigate and develop alternatives. Personal empowerment is infectious. It has the effect of helping others see new things as possible and inspiring them to act on that insight.

To reclaim our power we need to examine our beliefs about power. It is a very misused concept, which is currently being questioned and redefined by many groups, including the women's movement and ecological thinkers.

Personal power leading to people power can be contrasted with what we generally think of when we hear the term "power" — that is, power which is conferred through structural power or "power over". These forms of power give the ones at the top the right and/or might to force others to do what they want them to do. This is not the case with personal or people power, which is much more fluid, synergistic, cooperative and indirect.

"The denial of power is as endemic to our culture as the denial of feelings."
— Kevin McVeigh.

So if we potentially have personal power, why is it that we often have trouble expressing it?

There are many reasons. It would be simplistic not to acknowledge that some individuals and groups have a much longer journey, against greater resistance, towards the realization of their personal power than others. Those who experience more oppression, such as women and minority groups, have many more layers of resistance to get through. These layers are both external and internal — because oppressive beliefs easily become internalized. Not only do we come to believe the oppressive attitudes and limitations and accept them as reality, but furthermore we perpetuate them by limiting others.

Often the experiences we have as young people actively set up this pattern of self-limitation. A friend, Denise Nagorka, described her insights:

PAST EXPERIENCES

"When I was growing up, I did recognize that I was experiencing things differently from the big people around me. A lot of my energy went into trying to protect myself and avoid harassment. I had no models that

said: 'If you don't like things you can change them'. What I realize is
that inside myself that dialogue sometimes continues — I still think I'm
back there, when I hear myself say : 'Don't stick your neck out, sit quietly,
then you won't get criticized'."

Growing up in our culture usually does little to prepare us for responding
appropriately to problems of this magnitude. Most social institutions, and
the education system in particular, encourage us to conform to the existing
social systems rather than think we can change them. We are taught what
is acceptable to think and do. Rocking the boat, questioning authority,
or upsetting established structural power relationships is definitely not
encouraged! "It is impolite to disagree. The experts and powerholders
know what is best for us." "Avoid being in a situation that would bring
disapproval."

We are not encouraged to trust our perceptions, feelings and judgments
— especially if they are out of sync with the status quo. This combination
of pressures is usually enough to keep us immobilized — even if we do
have a queasy feeling that it isn't right.

When we wake up to the reality of how powerlessness is drummed
into us, everything begins to change. Denise continues:

"When I realized this, through talking with people, particularly in groups,
I was able to start acting differently. When my daughter says :'I don't
like it', we take the time to look at options: how can this be changed?
It is a bit like watching the way water flows off dirt roads; you watch
the way it normally goes, then you give it a new channel to flow in."

Feelings of powerlessness will expand or contract depending on our
notion of how change happens.

CHANGE MYTHS AND BELIEFS

What do you tell yourself about what it would take to change things?

We are often guided by myths. If we believe that change is initiated
only by the leaders — the men, the big shots, the ones who make the
rules — or only by pulling strings on high, and pushing others around,
then we are not likely to feel part of it.

However, if we see considerable change happening from the bottom
up — the accumulation of individuals taking action and making moment-
to-moment choices — we will know that we have a role to play in it.
As Fran Peavey says in her inspiring book *Heart Politics:* "I act on the
conviction that everyone is making a difference. Just by living our lives,
consuming space and resources, we are making a difference. Our choice
is what kind of difference to make."[1]

We make a difference by exercising our consumer choice, by the quality
of contact with friends and neighbors or by building vitality and integrity

into our own lives, our family, and our community. As M.K. Gandhi said so simply:

"Almost anything you do will seem insignificant, but it is very important that you do it."

I can have the experience of making a difference by starting with the nearest thing. This experience also builds confidence for larger projects such as forming groups, organizing campaigns and exercising leadership.

As a participant at an empowerment workshop put it: "At first I thought I had to completely reorganize my life, wait for the kids to grow up, get the mortgage paid off, before I could start... but then I saw I could just start from where I was."

The idea of the "Hundredth Monkey" has been an important (if clichéd) guiding myth of our times. (Even if the details of the tale are inaccurate). This myth stemmed from reports of the behavior of groups of monkeys on some isolated islands, who started to wash their sweet potatoes. This was taught to the younger monkeys in the group until many of the monkeys were doing it. The story goes that at one point monkeys on a relatively nearby, but isolated, island — monkeys who had not had contact with the first group — also began to wash their sweet potatoes.

The basic idea is that when enough people have a change of consciousness, reaching a critical mass, they can bring about a sudden change in the wider society. The momentous changes in Eastern Europe are a good example of this.

Another inspiring guiding myth is that of the ripple effect outlined in *The Tao of Leadership:*[2]

"A ripple effect works because everyone influences everyone else.

Powerful people are powerful influencers.

If your life works, you influence your family.

If your family works, your family influences the community.

If your community works, your community influences the nation.

If your nation works, your nation influences the world."

Another motivating belief is based on the notion that where the people lead, the leaders will follow. If enough strategic moral and popular pressure is demonstrated (at least in a democracy), then the powerholders will eventually have to adopt the line. As former US President Eisenhower once said:

"I like to believe that people, in the long run, are going to do more to promote peace than governments. Indeed, I think that people want peace so much that one of these days governments had better get out of their way and let them have it."

"Powerful people are powerful influences."
— *John Heider.*

This can be demonstrated over and over again to be the case with changes of policy where politicians jump in front of a strong trend of public opinion and attempt to make it look as though they are initiating the changes or had intended to all along. (President Reagan's change of heart towards the Soviet Union is a good example.) It can be very empowering to educate each other on how historical events that led to major changes did in fact unfold — and to validate the role of citizen-led social movements.

It is fruitful to question whether your belief system about how change happens is likely to sustain you in positive action. Relying on mainstream media for information about change can discourage personal involvement in social change because of the selective emphasis on high profile personalities or institutions and the focus on problems and disasters. It is hard to gain a perspective on individual contributions to the slow building of change, or of unspectacular but solid achievements being made.

DISEMPOWER-ING BELIEFS

It is empowering to focus on the everyday heroism of small actions.

What is your notion of what is required of you? If you perceive that to be responsible enough, adequate enough, you have to be a heroic activist, one who makes bold gestures against incredible obstacles, and who speaks eloquently to very large groups, then you may have trouble identifying with this. We certainly need our heroes and heroines; however it seems most of them start out quite small.

Jo Valentine, as a Green Independent member of the Federal Senate in Australia — in fact the first Senator elected on an anti-nuclear platform — described to me how she started:

"The first thing I did after the birth of my first child was to organize a babysitting group in the neighborhood. It was a sanity saver. I had been involved in community groups before that time but this was the first thing I did from scratch by myself. I just decided — this is important. I wheeled the baby up and down the street and stopped anyone else who had a baby and asked 'What do you do about babysitters?' A lot of them said, 'Oh well, we just don't go out — we've got no parents around so that is just how it is.' I'd heard of these babysitting groups before and I rang a few to find out how they worked. Then I thought, 'Heck, if I can do that, well what next?' So I began to take on the city council — trying to get our area declared a nuclear free zone."

Another common disempowering belief is the tyranny of the idea of "The Expert". Carol, a workshop participant, said:

"I was intimidated by thinking I needed to know a lot about nuclear weapons in order to speak out about them. I knew the basics — it was clearly madness! I woke up to the fact that I had been giving my consent by my silence, and my non-involvement." This, however, should not discourage you from training and informing yourself to increase your effectiveness.

Having an exaggerated sense of awe about people in power can also be an obstacle. Richard Jones, Member of Parliament in the Upper House in NSW, told me: "The first realization must be that the Prime Minister, members of the Royal Family, the Premier — indeed anybody in public positions like that — are ordinary people, just like you or I. It's just that they have found themselves in unusual circumstances. They don't regard themselves as anything but ordinary. Don't look up to them, look at them on the level . . . It makes a big difference."

SELF-CRITICISM

It is not only our perceptions of others that may need to change — our perceptions of ourselves may need to change also. Many of us are in the habit of perpetual self-criticism, often quite unconsciously. Another foundation for empowerment is to make a commitment to stop devaluing ourselves and instead to learn to affirm ourselves and others. In counseling clients, I often observe that the idea of stopping this internal harassment initially comes as a great surprise. But once the connection is made that being criticized by others in childhood leads to learning to criticize oneself, then clients see that this is something they can take some control over. Consequently more and more focus can be put on the positives, affirming the differences we do make and the things we do well. It sounds simple, but it takes great persistence.

James Bennett-Levy described how, when he was part of a support group, they used to ask each other: "How have you changed the world today?" At first the idea seemed ridiculous, confronting or even absurd. But the effect of hearing the answers was very encouraging . . . "I resolved a dispute with my neighbor". "I said no thanks, I won't use plastic bags". "I stopped to chat and smile at the man who sold the tickets, I left him feeling good . . . he probably smiled at the next 10 people."

TRANS-FORMING FEAR

Fear is the basic emotion that acts as the brake. It can be very liberating to form a different relationship with feelings of fear: "Feel the fear but do it anyway."

Nan Nicolson described her experience on the Terania Creek Logging Blockade: "When I was confronted with trying to get my first media interview, it was only the passion for the cause that allowed me to contemplate doing it. I was driven by the realization that the media coverage was essential and someone had to do it. What got me over the hurdle was the knowledge that however ghastly, it would not last for ever. From that I learnt I could make a difference when I confronted my fear. Now I know how desperate TV, radio, and newspapers are for stories and how it is relatively easy to get covered when you hand the story over on a plate."

Moya Farrell, a peace and social justice activist from Newcastle, talked about how reframing what she was experiencing made a big difference for her. "While I still feel the fear, I don't let it stop me now. I see it as a pointer for work I need to do with myself, rather than something to make me say 'no, I shouldn't'. I tell myself that this is excitement — fear and excitement are very close feelings. I breathe with it a little — it helps!"

So rather than perceiving power as something people (ie. others) are born or blessed with, the focus can be on personal empowerment as a continual process of taking steps from where we are, taking steps to create and contribute towards how we want things to be, both inwardly and outwardly.

"Until one is committed, there is a hesitancy, the chance to draw back, always ineffectiveness.
"Concerning all acts of initiative (and creation), there is one elementary truth, the ignorance of which kills countless ideas and splendid plans: that the moment one definitely commits oneself, then Providence moves too.
"All sorts of things occur to help one that would never otherwise have occurred. A whole stream of events issues from the decision, raising in one's favor all manner of unforeseen incidents and meetings and material assistance, which no person could have dreamed would have come their way.
"Whatever you can do or dream you can, begin it.
Boldness has genius, power and magic in it. Begin it now."

— Goethe.

Making a Difference

EXERCISES

Relax, close your eyes and remember a time when you felt that some action you took made a difference that was positive. What happened? Who was involved? What was the setting? Remember as vividly as possible the qualities of mind and feelings you had at the time.

Either write this down for yourself or share your stories in a small group or in pairs.

Create an Empowerment Collage

This exercise is similar to the previous one, but uses different methods. Some people respond better in a non-verbal mode.

Close your eyes and relax. Let images float up of events, sources of inspiration and people that contribute to a sense of empowerment for you.

Now draw or paint something which represents these images. No artistic merit is needed.

If you are doing this as a group exercise, take a few minutes to share your collage. Keep it on your wall to remind you.

Good News Scrap-book

Neither the mainstream media nor our everyday gossip gives us much of a picture of the positive changes that individuals and grass-roots groups bring about. Our attitude is also often colored by the most recent so-called "major news story". The purpose of this exercise is to keep a reference of stories that remind us that individual actions do make a positive difference.

Start a paste-in scrap-book of inspirational stories and good news. Put in this scrap-book reports of successful projects from newspapers or newsletters. Write in accounts of your own stories, poems or titles of inspirational books or films. When you feel tempted to succumb to hopelessness, pull it out and leaf through it.

This sort of scrap-book makes a good family activity. Bobbi Allen, a friend of mine, decided to start good news scrap-books for her twin children to give to them on their 13th birthdays.

Critic Shrinking

Collusion with our internalized self critic is ultimately the main force in our disempowerment. This exercise is a fun way to shrink it or befriend it, and helps to develop resources for not taking the inner critical, doubting dialogue so seriously. It can be done alone. It is also good to do in groups of 4–6, taking it in turns. Keep the tone light and very irreverent!

Answer these questions either by yourself or with your group.
The group can help you with suggestions at any point if you get stuck.

- **What does your critic look like? Make the image as clear as you can. Characterize it, exaggerate it.**

- **What does it feel like when you listen to it? How does your body respond internally — for instance where do you feel tension building up? Exaggerate how your posture and expression changes.**

- **What sort of things is it saying when you wish to act on your inner convictions?**

Now have someone role play your critic, saying the things it says to you.

Play with creative ways to diminish its power and to answer back. Explore ways to release the tension build-up in your body.

Sometimes the most effective way to silence or diminish an inner critic is not to be violent or totally rejecting of it but rather to make some peace with it, be irreverent or better still turn it into an ally. For instance, one workshop participant found that her internal critic turned into a fairly whining kid that just needed a hug and a dummy. Another acknowledged that although his made it hard to write, the critic made a wonderful editor.

- **How could you turn your critic into an ally? In what aspects of your work is it useful?**
- **Spend the last few minutes firming an image, symbol or a gesture which sums up your new attitude towards your critic. You can use this image again any time you need it.**

Some examples are: one woman experienced her critic as a hammer which kept hitting her head, so she then visualized putting on a fancy padded shower cap so it no longer had an impact. Another person enjoyed blowing raspberries and poking out her tongue to the grey-bearded dour old man on her shoulder. Another experienced it as a greeny-grey gloop on his shoulders and feet, so he scraped it off and rolled it in balls and playfully threw it away.

Skills and Resources   The purpose of this exercise is to remember and validate skills and resources that we have to contribute in our work for social change. It can also encourage you to take a wider view of what you have to offer and to highlight things you especially love to do. This is an opportunity to include your whole self, rather than selecting certain more acceptable parts, as we may be inclined to do when making job applications. Don't prejudge what is needed or is relevant; all sorts of skills are vital to the composite process of social change. The things we feel a passion for will be our greatest source of energy.

This exercise can be done individually, although it would be useful to share your results with others later. A friend who knows you well could assist you to include assets you may be overlooking. It is a long exercise, so allow at least 30 minutes for the first section and 30 minutes more if you do part two.

PART ONE

● Take a few moments to relax and get comfortable.

● On a very large sheet of paper start to create a "brain-net". This is a loose association of ideas, which flow uncensored into clusters. Create 4 quadrants on the page.

On one, write down all the SKILLS you might have to offer (eg. ability to organize information, parenting, scrounging for cheap things, listening skills etc.)

In another corner write down those EXPERIENCES that have contributed to developing your skills (eg. worked in a library, campaigned for a school crossing, lived in a share house, acted as treasurer for a social group etc.)

In another corner create a net of the RESOURCES you have which may be useful (eg. a car, phone, good links in the neighborhood, a house where meetings could be held, etc.)

In the remaining corner write down POSITIVE PERSONAL QUALITIES which will be useful in achieving your goals (eg. tenacious, get on well with most people, learn quickly, assertive). Don't censor or reject things as irrelevant and keep adding more until you run out of possibilities.

EXAMPLE OF A BRAIN-NET:

```
┌─────────────────────────────────┬─────────────────────────────────┐
│  Letter writing  Typing  Listening +      Friendly with    ┌House for meetings
│              └─shorthand communication   parents and teachers
│                      Conflict ┘          in district┐      ┌Babysitter
│                      Resolution
│         ┌─────────────────┐              ┌─────────────────┐
│         │     SKILLS       │              │    RESOURCES     │
│         └─────────────────┘              └─────────────────┘
│  Organizing        Research/Info    Car                      Typewriter
│  People            gathering
│                                                        └Friend who works
│                                          Phone +         in public relations
│            Parenting                     Answer machine   firm
├─────────────────────────────────┼─────────────────────────────────┤
│         ┌Working in an  Parents +       Well organized  Persistent ┌Get on well
│          office        Teachers                                     with most
│  Library work         Association       Good at detailed           people
│                                         work┐
│         ┌─────────────────┐              ┌─────────────────┐
│         │   EXPERIENCES    │              │+ PERSONAL QUALITIES│
│         └─────────────────┘              └─────────────────┘
│  Campaign for          Public          Care about
│  school crossing       speaking        my community    Have a calming
│            Petition                    + family        influence in
│  Lobbying  signature                                   conflict situations
│            gathering
└─────────────────────────────────┴─────────────────────────────────┘
```

- The next step is to look at the net and draw links between related items, perhaps group some together, or delete repetitions. Rearrange it until you can see some patterns emerging.
- Highlight with a colored pen the things you especially love to do, or things that are more highly developed. In another color mark things you do not want to do, or roles you are sick of.
- Next ask yourself: what does this particular set of skills and experiences suggest about your potential? What specifically do you have to offer?

PART TWO

- Use what you have written in the brain-net to write yourself a long, general reference in the third person — a reference stating why you are a suitable person for a particular job you wish to occupy or a general purpose reference on what you have to offer for healing the world. Read these to each other in pairs.

- Design yourself a perfect social action role that takes into account your unique skills and concerns. Even if you cannot immediately see how you could put this into effect now, let yourself expand your vision.

You could either ask yourself these questions alone or use them as the basis of a discussion group.

Empowerment Stories

● **What things have helped you realize you can bring about changes in your own life and in the wider world?**

● **How do you disempower yourself? How do you perceive others as doing this?**

● **Do you have a myth, belief or story that helps you put the current times in perspective, and to persist when the going gets rough?**

NOTES
1. Fran Peavey (with Myra Levy & Charles Varon), *Heart Politics*, New Society Publishers, Philadelphia, 1986.

2. John Heider, *The Tao of Leadership*, Humanics Publishing Group, P.O. Box 7447, Atlanta, Georgia, 1985.

CHAPTER THREE
Sustaining and Nourishing Action

Once we awaken to the reality of the world's problems, and recognize that our actions can make a difference, we are then faced with finding ways to nourish and sustain those actions. In the past, when staying involved with social change work has felt too hard, I have returned to four basic principles to replenish my resources to continue. These principles are: envisioning the future, reawakening hope and faith, finding ways to nourish my inner being and strengthening my sense of community.

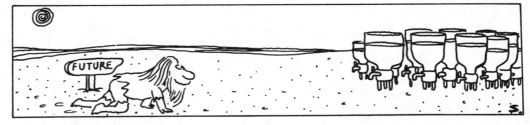

ENVISIONING

"When life itself seems lunatic, who knows where madness lies?... To surrender dreams this may be madness... too much sanity may be madness, and maddest of all is to see life as it is and not as it could be." Despite his delusory lunges at windmills, Don Quixote's words are pertinent.

It is hard to work for something that you cannot imagine. It is not enough to know what you do not want, nor to endlessly protest the status quo. To do so is to act out of a continual reactive mode which is exhausting, demoralizing and uncreative. It is like playing the other team's game.

We need to bring new circumstances into being. The first step in this creative process is being able to imagine vividly the desired result, as if it had already happened. This is the envisioning process.

We do in fact often use this ability to envision. We envision what it would be like to be with our beloved, to have children, to make our homes, what we will do when we win the lottery... We can use this same ability to tackle the complex and serious challenges that face us. This is not idle daydreaming; nor is it magical thinking that assumes picturing it will manifest it.

Envisioning is essential in order to widen our sense of what is possible, and to enhance our strategies for reaching from here to there. There is of course the continual challenge of translating the vision into reality. When we envision, we picture in vivid detail how we would wish things to be at a specific time in future, then retrace step by step, envisioning how that transition happened. Who needed to do what, what had to be readjusted, what had to get invented ?

This willingness to envision better things takes courage. It also takes energy to unglue ourselves from the mesmerization of the way things appear to be, and therefore will continue to be.

One reason positive visions are important is that we are bombarded with many negative scenarios of the future. It is reflected in so many aspects of literature, art, films. There is plenty of horrific doomsday information about what will happen if we continue in the current direction. If we take this as implying inevitability, then our only options are to get lost in short term hedonistic distraction, or to be faced with a pervasive sense of meaninglessness and despair.

Envisioning the future also gives us a framework for evaluating the present, whether on an individual basis or by groups who have defined their common vision.

> How is what I am doing now an expression of how I want it to be?
>
> What am I doing that is building towards my goals?
>
> What am I doing that is moving me away from my visions?
>
> Does the vision help integrate seemingly separate and competing aspects of my life? Does it help break down the compartments, so I can perceive a wholeness?

To live with a vision we are faced with the apparent paradox of also remaining flexible — to find creative ways to integrate others' dreams with our own, to ask ourselves: how does my vision also allow for individual diversity? Who is getting left out of my ideal world? Is there room in my dreams for all kinds of people? How will there be space for all the other life forms with whom I share this planet? This is surely one of the central puzzles to solve.

How can we sustain our actions and continue in the face of great uncertainty?

Fran Peavey told an Indian myth at an Interhelp Gathering that speaks to our situation. It is about the huma bird:.. "a magical creature that never touches the ground. It eats, sleeps, hunts and mates in flight high in the stratosphere, and there the mother lays her egg. The helpless new

SUSTAINING HOPE AND FAITH

"...The old is dead
and we don't quite
know what new thing
is being born in our
time." — Fran
Peavey.

egg plunges toward earth. But inside, an embryo is rapidly taking form: feet, head, wings. Its beak hardens, it pecks at the shell and finally emerges to find itself hurtling like a meteor towards disaster. As the ground looms even larger, it finds its little wings drying out, unfolding. In the last split second before annihilation, it flaps those tiny new wings and flies up into the heavens."

Fran goes on to say: "I suppose you feel like the huma bird as often as I do these days. How are we going to get out of the egg of our despair and spiritual immaturity? Will our beaks harden in time? Will our wings dry out? We are right in the middle of that period when we can see the old is dead and we don't quite know what new thing is being born in our time."

Perhaps the short-term gains and immediate breakthroughs will be obvious and this will be enough to sustain you; or the transformations in your own life and in others close to you, will give you inspiration to continue. However, a lot of the changes won't necessarily be visible: the scale may be too large or the time too long for you to notice small, imperceptible shifts. There may be many setbacks, and a dark time before there is any visible result. Waiting without knowing is a painful reality of these times.

Can we make a shift to a firm place deep down inside us that allows us to continue, whether we see the results or not — to just keep joyfully doing what we do anyway. Our motivation might be: "I would do this anyway, even if this doesn't work, even if my/our efforts fail. This is a way of being and living life that is an expression of values I believe in." Here we have an expression of faith in the intrinsic integrity of the process.

As one empowerment workshop participant put it: "Life has taken on a deeper meaning; a sense of dignity and consequence has been added, way beyond what my life would have been if I had just kept my focus on my family and my immediate life. I feel like I am expressing something very basic about the value of life and living."

One thing that gives me hope and faith is observing how life seems infinitely regenerative. When toxic and life-destroying influences are removed, the intrinsic life force takes care of the rest. In my work as a counselor and groupleader, over and over again I have observed the innate drive we have to reach out and care for each other. It seems it is not something that we need to learn; we only need to heal the pain and distress (leading to fear) that gets in the way — a basic human drive for cooperation then blossoms.

I am encouraged to see how other life forms never give up. I was in jail for obstructing a bulldozer during a mineral sands mining operation at Middle Head on the Central NSW Coast. I had seen the bulldozer drivers knocking down ancient forest on the edge of the dunes to get at the sands. We'd lost the campaign, jail was barren and I was desolate. Jail was a symbol of punishment goading me to desert what I saw was right. Time passed slowly and the sandwiches were appalling.

My mood suddenly lifted when I looked up and saw a fern growing in the high brick wall beside me. A toehold in a crack was sufficient for the life force to reassert itself! I had the feeling at the time that the fern and I understood each other.

Being around people with a positive outlook will of course have a big influence. This is enhanced when there is involvement with support networks and a community of like-minded people — a topic which is developed later in this section.

When 5 per cent of society accepts an idea it becomes "embedded".

Another perspective to keep in mind is that the first stages in changing society's attitudes are invariably the hardest. Dr Everett Rogers and his co-workers at the University of Southern California have shown in their research that when 5 per cent of society accepts an idea, it becomes "embedded". Prior to this point, proponents of the new idea must work incessantly just to keep the idea alive. It takes additional work and steady effort till it is accepted by approximately 20 per cent of the population at which point it generally becomes unstoppable.[1]

Kerith Power, a singer, songwriter and preschool teacher, said: "What I have realized from being involved with social change for many years now, is the need to be really, really persistent. That never changes. I have to be persistent against messages from others who say: 'Well that's never been done before.' It's as if that means it cannot be! Being around young people is what keeps my hope alive."

There are new beings born every moment who are fresh and completely open to a new approach, if they are given the chance. It is only from within the human psyche that our present problems ultimately stem; only habits of mind are creating the limitations that curtail the changes we need to make.

NOURISHING OUR INNER BEINGS — CARING FOR WHOLENESS

Solving the problems that face the planet at this critical time will not be done in a quick burst of frantic action by anyone — "Quick clever fixes from smart tense people".[2] Sometimes I find myself thinking "I'll just get through this project/campaign, then get on with my life." But I remind myself that I'll probably still be doing this when I reach 60. So it comes down to finding ways of living our lives with a sense of wholeness and sustainability.

"Can healing the earth be a delight? Will it ever happen if it isn't?" asks Ann Herbert.[3]

Have you had a conversation with an activist that goes something like this?:

"Hi! How are you going?"

"Dreadful, really tired."

"What's been happening?"

"Going to meetings, doing blah, blah ... Never stops."

"How about we get together sometime?"

"Let's see, I'll check the diary ... No, not for about four weeks"

"OK. If that is when you can."

"Can't see why more don't come to our ..."

Sounds like fun, eh! Whoopee — can't wait to join the life style!

Unfortunately, too many activists fall prey to burnout. It takes its insidious toll physically, emotionally and in relationships, not to mention the cost of lessened effectiveness. We become disillusioned, embittered and frustrated because the needs of the inner being are ignored. These needs have a way of insisting, eventually, to be met. It is ironic that while many dedicated people are passionately trying to bring about wholeness, justice and sustainability in the outer world, in their inner worlds there may be fragmentation, injustice and oppression.

While I was thinking about writing this section I dreamt of camels. Sometimes the journey can feel like crossing arid lands. Camels need to drink deeply, to store up inner nourishment to sustain their journeys between wells and oases. They also chew their cud and have times of gazing dispassionately into the distance.

> Ask yourself: What, or who in my life are my wells?
> Where are my oases?
> What nourishment do I need to keep body and soul going, for the long haul?

On this theme and its relationship to burnout prevention — planning strategies for personal and group burnout prevention — see the last section of this book.

BUILDING COMMUNITY — CARING FOR EACH OTHER

One of the most empowering and liberating discoveries I have made is that I do not have to meet these challenges alone. It is not about sterling individual efforts of epic proportions. (The prospect of such labors feels daunting enough to keep me paralyzed.) Instead I have experienced the tremendous support, learning and context for action that comes from building community.

People living in modern, western — particularly urban — societies often need to do this building quite consciously and deliberately. Unless we are fortunate enough to live or grow up in a fairly intact community, most of us are easily alienated from each other.

I have noticed in my work as a counselor that the most disempowered are also the most isolated. In this isolation they are very susceptible to the conditioning of powerlessness with which our society relentlessly irrigates us. In working with these people the path is one of rebuilding solid connections with other people — to let relationships blossom, and through that, a new sense of a self that belongs and responds by making choices in life.

The same principle applies on a much wider scale. So many successful nonviolent movements grow out of the soil of "base communities". Examples are: the Ghandi campaign against the British in India, the women's movement and the anti-nuclear lobby.

These "base communities" don't have to take a particular form, though structuring them deliberately to meet particular needs can be very effective in supporting sustained social action, as discussed in the chapter on support and accountability groups. These groups need not be residential or elitist, nor have a rigid ideology — though obviously, a sense of shared values is important cement.

Projects grow through personal contacts.

What is required to build community is a sense of mutual commitment to each other, a willingness to assist each other's empowerment, to foster honest, caring relationships that are not just task oriented, but rather ones that are interested in the wholeness of each member.

I have experienced the richness that comes from appreciating, in community, people from diverse backgrounds, with different talents, who are at different stages of life. Some of us are getting born, some growing up, some dying. Some of us are focussed on raising children and the politics of the home front. Some of us are focussed on political work in the green movement or in community development. But there are many ways to affirm and practically support each other: babysitting, financial support, planning time, counseling, transport, or some honest feedback.

ONLY "US" HERE — NO MORE "THEMS"

How often have you secretly held the notion that we are the ones working on "the real issue"? — it's a pity about all these other misguided people! Being involved in community helps keep a sense of the whole in perspective — though for now you may be focussing on one part. Turning this crisis around will take lots of us working from all sorts of angles and adopting many different roles.[4]

Community also provides the context from which to initiate and collaborate on projects. Very few things are successful when they are done from a base of isolation. Over and over it has been my experience that it is through the personal contacts that projects grow. From already knowing and trusting each other, thoughts come into form; the push comes to take another little step and dreams become reality.

Make room for lizards, wombats, owls and grizzly bears!

Within community we can experience the truth of our interdependence, and also learn to trust our "Power With". We can see how the sum of our actions is more than the addition of individual efforts. However, being involved in community requires us to continually rub off the rough edges: the fear, the competitiveness, the conflict. It is through resolving these issues, learning the skills of conflict resolution, and loving each other in our diversity, that we are melting the core of the fundamental problems in our wider human family. From that grows the sense that there is only "Us" here — no "Thems".

In a wider sphere, building a sense of community means embracing other species, other life forms, making room in the sense of "Us" for lizards, wombats, owls and grizzly bears. From this awareness destructive habits get questioned and changed, and we are more empowered to work on behalf of all life forms.

Finally, no chapter dealing with issues such as sustaining hope and faith, nourishing our inner being or building community can be complete without touching on the role of spiritual beliefs and practices.

For many, spiritual beliefs and practice, in the widest sense, are the wellspring for experiencing a sense of relatedness to a larger whole, beyond the boundaries of the individual ego. Spiritual practice opens us to sources of guidance and solace in adversity. It also develops perspectives that can encompass the complexities and contradictions in which engaging in social change work embroils us.

EXERCISES

What Sustains Me

This exercise can be done on your own or you can take it in turns to talk about the following questions in a small group.

1. **What sustains you in your work for social change, especially when the results are not yet apparent?**
   Or if you are new to the field of social action:
   What has worked to sustain you in other circumstances in your life?
2. **What do you need to enable you to keep going?**
3. **What can you do in the next 24 hours to contribute to this?**

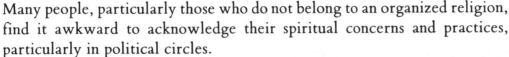

Acknowledging Our Spiritual Practice

Many people, particularly those who do not belong to an organized religion, find it awkward to acknowledge their spiritual concerns and practices, particularly in political circles.

The purpose of this exercise is to break down the artificial barriers we create between different parts of our lives. This exercise has an implicit assumption that participants have some form of spiritual beliefs and/or practice. (If any participants object to this assumption, you could suggest they talk instead on why spirituality is not relevant for them.)

In pairs Partner A takes 2–3 minutes to answer each question while Partner B listens attentively. Then swap over. This could lead on to a general group discussion on the relationship of spirituality to social action.

1. **What does spirituality mean for you?**
2. **How does this enhance your work for peace, justice, the environment, etc.?**
3. **Assuming you do have spiritual concerns or a spiritual practice, how do you feel about it, and how do you "come out" about it? To family, friends, in your workplace, or in social action circles?**

On Being Supported — A Guided Meditation

Sometimes activists take the attitude of struggling on alone and perceive that they are unsupported, even when this is not true. This can increase stress and contribute to burnout. The purpose of this meditation is to help decrease the feeling of isolation and to enhance the perception of being part of a larger whole. It validates the support we receive just from being alive on this earth; it doesn't replace the need, however, to set up links and support networks of appropriate people.

This exercise can be done with someone cradling your neck with one hand, which increases the experience of being supported and is often effective to relieve stress. (A leader would need to assess whether this cradling and the content of the meditation were appropriate for a particular group.) If you choose to do the neck cradling, one person lies down while another sits behind and places a hand firmly but gently behind the neck, taking the weight of the head just slightly. Encourage people to find a position they can hold for 15 minutes or so without straining their backs.

Lie down in a comfortable position... loosen any tight clothing... let your whole body relax... feel your body getting heavier... there is no effort needed, you are supported by the earth beneath you... passively give in to gravity... supported by the earth below... (Pause)

Notice your breathing... in... out... in effortless cycles... you are supported by the air... life-giving oxygen... taking away your carbon dioxide... in... out... keep relaxing... (Pause)

Notice the feeling of your clothes against your skin... keeping in your warmth... keeping you comfortable... (Pause)

Tune into a deeper level inside your body..there are thousands of processes going on in there... your heart is circulating your blood... your digestive system is breaking down food... cells repairing tissue... (Pause)... processes in your body always trying to bring you into a state of health and balance... this just continues effortlessly... feel the miracle of that... (Pause)

Be aware of the nourishment you take in... your last meal being transformed into your substance and energy... (Pause)... think of the countless animals... plants and microbes which have contributed to supporting you... endlessly cycling molecules... the sunlight... the soil all supporting you... (Pause)

Let yourself become aware of the humans who have supported you... as a baby in your mother's womb... later caring for and feeding you countless times... (Pause)... bring to mind an image of one person who has particularly loved and cared for you... remember that loving concern... breathe that in... (Pause)... remember others who have also supported you... wished you well... remember their voices, their touch, what it felt like to be with them... keep breathing that in... perhaps teachers, or friends you have learnt things from... who support you... bring to mind your loving response to that... let yourself feel deeply that support... (Pause)

Widen your awareness to encompass other powers that create and support life... support you... whatever you visualize that to be... it may be a sense of a presence... keep breathing that in... stay with the awareness of that... let the tangible feeling and knowing of all these levels of support seep right down into your cells... (Pause)

(Partners who have been cradling can move aside quietly and begin to relax for their turn.)

When you are ready, start to wiggle your toes... open your eyes... roll over... and start to move (perhaps crawl) around the room... go very slowly and stay with the feelings you have had... give simultaneous attention to sensing inside and outside yourself... slowly crawl around the room.. interacting gently with others nonverbally... let in the support that is here in the room for you...

(After the second turn, if done in pairs, suggest participants find their partners and share what that exercise was like for them both.)

Your Support-Community Collage

Many of us have a tendency to feel isolated at one time or another. The purpose of this exercise is to have a concrete reminder of who your community of supporters is. I used this when I went away from home for a few months to complete the writing of this book. Each time I felt stuck I would look up at the photos above my desk of the people who I knew wished me to succeed in my task.

- On a large sheet of paper or cardboard, create a collage of the people in your support community. Use photos, drawings or something else which represents individuals and groups who support you.
  If you find this exercise difficult or your collage remains rather empty, take this time to identify what this feels like. Ask yourself:

- How does it affect what I do or don't do?

- What kinds of people would I like to actively build relationships with? (See Chapter 10 for ideas on setting up a support group.)

  If you are doing this exercise in a group:
- Share your collage and what you discovered by doing this exercise with a small group.

NOTES
1. Dr Everett Rogers, *Beyond War* Newsletter, June, 1986, p 4. Quoted in "The Vision That Connects — Building The Future We Choose," transcript of a lecture given by Carol & Dougald McLean for Religious Society of Friends, Australia, 1987.

2. Ann Herbert, "Let the Good Times Last", *Awakening in the Nuclear Age Journal*, 1986.

3. Ann Herbert, *ibid*.

4. Bill Moyer in *The Practical Strategist* (see *Suggested Reading*) has a very useful model for understanding and appreciating the often apparently contradictory roles needed to be played by change agents in different positions, at different stages of social movements.

CHAPTER FOUR
Insight as a Resource

~~~

Have you ever had "your buttons pressed", in a way that seemed very out of proportion to the situation?

Do you get filled with bouts of righteous zeal that would put the fundamentalists to shame?

Have you ever considered that you may have chosen a particular issue to focus on because it is reminiscent of some powerful experiences in your personal life or upbringing?

Insight into how our motives, reactions, and perceptions may distort and sabotage the best of campaigns is crucial if we wish to be effective. Awareness and insight into ourselves is perhaps the most important inner resource we can bring to the field of social action.

Vimila Thaker says: "The inner and the outer are delicately intertwined in a totality, and we cannot deal with the one successfully without the other. The structures and systems condition the inner consciousness, and the conditionings of the consciousness create the structure and systems. We cannot carve out one part of the relationship, make it bright and beautiful, and ignore the rest."[3]

Often I have observed in myself and others how easy it is for the personal, psychological agenda to intrude so strongly that our actions, perhaps initially taken with good intent, become counterproductive. This is illustrated by the following situation:

There was a demonstration in Lismore about a bulldozer clearing trees for a car park close to the river bank. A spontaneous delegation was formed of mainly local residents who decided to march to the local government council chambers to protest. The mood was highly charged with a good strong dose of righteous indignation. Much to the horror of some of the demonstrators, one person started up his chain saw in the council offices and threatened to saw the Town Clerk's desk if he didn't respond to the group's demands. The atmosphere was tense and volatile. This behavior jeopardized relationships with the council that had been carefully cultivated by the conservation lobby over a number of years. It also stopped any possibility of meaningful dialogue on the issue at the time.

THE REBEL

Our personalities are made up of many different sub personalities or roles. In Chapter 2 we discussed the disempowering effect of the internal critic which can be harsh on ourselves and others. Another aspect of our personalities — the Rebel — is also most useful to be aware of. (There are other common characters or roles that people in social change movements play out, such as Victim or Hero, but the one I notice often causing difficulties is the Rebel.) Often it is this rebel part which is activated when we realize we don't like what is happening and we want to stop it. It will react, for instance, against authority being used oppressively, or against unjust structures.

Initially the Rebel has a lot of positive qualities to offer. It gets us going, and is prepared to say a strong No! Rebels generally have a lot of energy, enjoy a fight and get great satisfaction in finding ways to beat the system. But the Rebel can trip us up as well. It can distort reality in a way that escalates conflict, as in the example above, or it can create an overly intense investment in the work with the danger of burnout.

Rebels also tend to be fairly unreceptive, rigid and unwilling to listen. They tend to react against any hint of rules or restrictions. Having an intense charge about the situation, they may contribute to unrealistic expectations about the pace of change. Often the energy of the Rebel is more invested in being rebellious than in being effective; it may even be more invested in maintaining the problem than in contributing to the solution.[4]

PROJECTIONS

In making a commitment to sustained social responsibility and action, it is important for us to untangle our unconscious personal motivations and psychological issues (eg. a general hatred of authority figures), from our conscious purposes (eg. saving the local community center). Unfortunately the entanglement of the two strands undermines and misdirects many otherwise well-intentioned efforts.

These unconscious motives mostly derive from our past history, usually from childhood experiences. They are what psychologists call "projections", because they are projected from the past onto the current situation, or from our inner world onto the outer world and they thereby distort reality.

Projection is a common trick of the mind. Projection may influence both what issues we choose to focus on, and the way we react to individuals and groups. We do this for three main reasons:

1. Parts of ourselves that we do not accept come to be seen as belonging to others. This allows us to react strongly to these traits, eg. seeing others as aggressive while not recognizing our own aggression.

2. Unresolved feelings from our past which are restimulated by the

Qualities get polarized when we take the moral high ground.

present situation, eg. feelings of intimidation by public officials could stem from old feelings of intimidation by our father or school teacher.

3. Unacknowledged personal needs distort our reactions, eg. reacting strongly when not feeling accepted or resenting others who are popular without recognizing why.

An example of the first type of projection is how especially intolerant we may be of qualities in others that we have ourselves but refuse to "own". This is illustrated by psychotherapist Hugh Crago: "If, as a radical activist, you are not able to admit to yourself how stuck you are in certain key areas of your personal life, how conservative, in fact, then you will be insufficiently respectful of the conservatism of others. You will be wanting to push for change in ways that are too speedy, too confronting, for most of the people you are addressing. Hence you can expect constant frustration in your work".[5]

Another example is how we create the concept of Us and Them. Qualities get polarized when we take the moral high ground. From there we go on to create The Enemy, possessing all evil qualities, while we possess only the good ones.

Unraveling the projection gives some room to move and allows relationships to build, as James Bennett-Levy discovered:

"I was in England in 1987 when Margaret Thatcher was returned as Prime Minister with yet another huge majority. For the previous eight years I had loathed her and everything she stood for. I regarded myself as a political exile in Australia. It was almost as if she were the personification of evil. Yet here was the population of my home country giving her still another resounding vote of confidence. Were they all deluded fools? I was forced to ask myself why she was so popular. And was she so incredibly evil?

"I came to recognize that, however misguided I considered her politics, she really cared for the country and believed that what she was doing was for the best. I also recognized that she did have some remarkable qualities — her persistence, her determination and her capacity for work, for example. From there, my attitude towards her supporters softened. I noticed I was able to get into some meaningful dialogues, rather than dismiss them instantly as idiots. I have even found myself saying to Labor Party supporters: "She must be doing some things right; maybe there are some things to be learnt from her."

The second reason for projection is that undealt-with feelings from our personal history create an out-of-proportion reaction to present situations.

Anthea Duquemin, who organized Peace activities in Darwin, described to me how being aware of this made a difference to her approach: "It was very illuminating seeing through my involvement with the anti-US Bases campaign. I'd get so fired up with indignation when explaining the presumptuousness of the USA in building bases on our land... Then in a flash I saw through it — it was my 'stuff' about power. Here was a chance for me to righteously vent all of my anger for all the times I felt powerless, and actually seem virtuous in the process. After that I remained involved but I had a different attitude."

The anger vented by many activists, though sparked by the lies or brutality of the present situation, is fuelled by inner resentment often dating back to early childhood.

The third basis for projection may come from unacknowledged emotional needs.

Undealt-with feelings create out-of-proportion reactions.

Tony Yarrow, a youth worker, describes resentment towards a colleague: "When we were working full on, Chris was taking some time out to relax and had arranged some massages. I was incensed! The thought just kept going round and round inside me: him being uncommited, letting the side down, how dare he... I was ready to pounce, even though he was actually keeping up with the organizing of the refuge project. Then it occurred to me that I hadn't allowed myself to relax as he had, and I needed to. I had been afraid that if I stopped, I would just fall apart."

We may distort or manipulate situations in an attempt to get our needs met. This can be quite inappropriate. For example someone who insists on getting into prominent positions might be motivated by an old need to be acknowledged by "Daddy".

I am not suggesting for a moment that we need to deal completely with these personal issues before we can authentically engage in social action. Nor do I promote the philosophy that says by finding an inner resolution to such conflicts, we will lose our sense of social responsibility and thereby take no action. This argument has been put forward in many guises. There may be a time however of drawing back and re-evaluating until one finds within oneself a new center to work from.

INTEGRATING DISOWNED PARTS

I have heard it said, "But I might lose my energy if I weren't angry..." The challenge is to use the passion and drive that may come from this source, transmuting it positively with the power of insight. Disowned parts, which have been reintegrated, give us flexibility and breadth to enable clear thinking, intuition and creative spontaneity.

Integrating our personalities through developing insight and embracing our disowned parts is a lifelong process. These unresolved issues are both a burden and a gift. They point to the inner work we need to do in order to make ourselves whole. They potentially heighten our sensitivity, and enable us, through our personal issues, to perceive more clearly and to feel more acutely the larger issues of our society. What is required of us is to untangle the two agendas. I acknowledge this is not always an easy process.

Untangling our projections may take a willingness to honestly investigate our motives and reactions and to notice warning signs such as:
- Intense immediate reactions — "Inflamed rather than informed".
- Very persistent feelings or thoughts that are out of proportion to the situation.
- Sense of obsession creeping in.
- An inkling that the current situation is reminding you of past situations, or people, that have unhappy associations for you.

This is the time to take a deep breath and put aside some time to look within for the hidden causes. It may be useful to ask people you trust to give you some feedback about how they perceive your reaction. At the same time it is important to realize that it is easy to collude with each other's projection.

Untangling may also require giving priority to dealing with unfinished personal business as it is uncovered. This can be through counseling, journal keeping, emotional release techniques or any other of the myriad of resources now available for dealing with emotional issues. This commitment to ourselves is not separate from building social justice and a sustainable future.

"The revolutions of the past... have focussed on a fragment, either the outer life of socioeconomic or political structures or the inner life of consciousness. Because the solutions focus on the partial, significant dynamics are ignored; the pretense is that they do not exist, but because they do and will not be ignored, they create great sorrow."[6] So says Vimila Thakar, an Indian spiritual teacher and political activist. To take responsibility for, and loosen the grip of our projection, is also striking at the root causes of the problems in the outer world. Think globally, act locally.

Back to the Rebel. It is, after all, a source of fun. Its mischievous creativity and wicked humor is a refreshing break from being "nice" all the time. It is also a great stress reliever. Why not indulge this in a contained sort of way? — for example through channeling the drama into some street theatre or joking in the privacy of your meetings about your wildest fantasy in the situation. But the difference is you know you are doing it, and you have the flexibility and awareness to choose the most constructive response when action is called for.

EXERCISES

Untangling Projection Checklist

When you realize you are having a strong, possible over-reaction to a situation you can ask yourself these questions:

- What does this situation remind me of? When have I had similar feelings?

- Who in particular does this remind me of?

- What am I expecting will happen?

- What are the familiar unresolved bad feelings?

- How is this situation or this person different from then?

- What skills and resources do I have now that I didn't have then?

- Who do I need to forgive — including myself — for the past situation, and in what way?

- What do I need to do to act powerfully and clearly in the present situation?

Breathing to Contain Reactions

Because strong feelings may get triggered in conflict or confrontational situations, it is useful to have tools which give you more choices than to automatically respond with the first impulse. Though that is sometimes appropriate, there are other times when being able to "breathe through" strong emotions, observe and learn more about them is the most constructive response. Practice on less intense emotions at first. (This technique of observing can be abridged and will assist your responses in the heat of the moment.)

Switch your attention to your breathing . . . just the simple in . . . out of the breath . . . either the feel of the air as it passes your nostrils or the feel of your belly rising and falling . . . keep coming back to this as your mind jumps off elsewhere . . .

Bring to mind something you have felt very strongly about recently... Remember that incident as vividly as you can and what you were feeling... Keep your attention on your emotions... Where in your body are you actually feeling this feeling now? ... is it a feeling of fear ... anger ... sadness ... or something else?

What are the sensations in your body associated with this feeling? ... do they change? ... Stay for awhile switching your attention between your breath and what you are feeling... wait for it to shift a little ... You may identify a deeper reason for the reaction... Keep paying attention to your breath until the feeling subsides. Or is it appropriate to identify someone with whom you could talk — which may help you to resolve it?

Getting to Know Your Rebel

The purpose of this exercise is to evaluate whether the role of "Rebel" enhances or detracts from your work for social change. It can be done alone or with someone reading the prompts to a group. Have sheets of paper and pens ready to jot down notes as you go.

Close your eyes and relax after each question.

- What things have you rebelled against (successfully or unsuccessfully) in your life?

- What sorts of situations, people or issues really "got you going"?

- Visualize an image of what your Rebel looks like. If it were a cartoon or movie character, who would he/she be like? How old do you feel when you get into this role?

- How much is it a part of your image of yourself?

- What positive qualities does this Rebel have to offer?

- What are the negative qualities? What ways does it stop you from responding appropriately in certain situations?

- What do you need to do to use the positive qualities but not sabotage your goals by reacting from this negative Rebel?

Discuss what you discovered in small groups of 3–4.

NOTES

1. Hugh Crago, "The Paradoxes of Change, What Can Social Activists Learn from the Experiences of Psychotherapists?", *Australian Society Magazine*, December 1984. I am indebted to Crago for the inspiration to write and some of the content of this chapter.

2. Hugh Crago, *ibid.*

3. Vimila Thakar, *Spirituality and Social Action*, Vimila Programs, California, 1984.

4. Bill Moyer has some very interesting examples of the different roles in social movements that can be played positively or negatively, namely: citizen, reformer, rebel, and change agent. In *The Practical Strategist* published by the Social Movement Empowerment Project. (See *Suggested Reading*.)

5. Hugh Crago, *ibid.*

6. Vimila Thakar, *ibid.*

Tools for Effectiveness

CHAPTER FIVE
Listening for Change

————————————————————————————

Can you remember a time when you felt really listened to? What difference did that make? Can this kind of total listening offer anything in our troubled world — a world that seems to cry out for decisive action? I believe it can and that it has proved to be a powerful tool for social change and empowerment.

High quality listening is potentially empowering for both the listener and the speaker. Being listened to in a way that allows the expression of doubts, confusions and half-formed ideas, can be a pivotal factor in coming to a sense of inner clarity and strength — which then leads to appropriate action. Such actions could be to speak up about toxic waste in the neighborhood, or simply to reach out to a neighbor in distress.

The simple yet powerful act of listening is relatively rare in our culture. Good listening is far from being passive; it requires alertness and energy.

There are qualities which distinguish good listening from the kind commonly experienced. Listening requires having a genuine interest in what the other has to offer, even if it is far from what we feel, or wish they were saying. It is this non-judgmental quality which creates the safety for a deeper exchange to take place; it allows the speaker to risk exposing the controversial, the unformed dreams and the unacknowledged conflicts that may be blocking action or producing counterproductive action.

Normally in conversation we are formulating our responses while the other is speaking. When listening as a practice, energy is focussed solely on hearing, leaving the formulation of a response till later, if at all. This different quality of attention is intuitively sensed by the other and responded to accordingly. Our body language, particularly eye contact, says a lot about our level of attention. (See summary of listening skills.)

Earl Koile, in his book *Listening As A Way Of Becoming*, writes: "Demanding clarity about thoughts and feelings before sharing them can be a real problem... What I need is to share my jumbled-up inner dialogue with someone who can hear, and in listening, can help me to hear myself. With help, I may find release from the captivity of my own words and touch delicate, frightening, or otherwise eclipsed feelings within me."

"The greatest compliment that was ever paid me was when one asked me what I thought and attended my answer." — Henry David Thoreau.

"Make a distinction between the person and their opinions — opinions are like clothes, a matter of taste and fashion that can be changed at will. Don't mistake them for the essential core."[1] — Mark Somner.

"I am more likely to risk letting out my thoughts and feelings if someone is not judging me right or wrong, consistent or inconsistent; not diagnosing and attaching labels; not pressing for logic or clarity. I do more than enough judging, labeling, and pressing for answers as I listen to myself. When I press too hard and doggedly for total understanding, I get too bottled up and stop up the sounds inside."[2]

"What I need is to share my jumbled-up inner dialogue with someone who can listen." — Earl Koile.

The changes and shifts that come about through being carefully listened to are not always apparent at the time. Frequently when people have an opportunity to hear themselves speak, changes will occur but time may be needed for the ideas to ferment.

A more active form of listening — also called reflective listening — can include feeding back what you hear in a way that affirms it has been received and is respected; this encourages the speaker to continue. This kind of listening is the essential element allowing and encouraging personal change in all the numerous types of psychotherapy and counselling. However, we do not need a lot of training in communication or therapy to be effective listeners.

To fully realize the inherent power of listening requires spaciousness — in the conversation, in a meeting or in one's life generally.

I have been enormously impressed by the New Zealand Maori tradition, which has infiltrated some sections of the Pakeha (white) culture, of coming together in large groups (sometimes over one hundred people) and having the patience and respect to be able to sit and listen until everybody who wishes to has spoken. Speaking is often followed by a song or a poem in the spirit of what they were saying. It can take days for full themes to emerge, for everyone to be included. (See speaking in council exercise.)

Western culture finds difficulty with space in every form, including the small silences and pauses that allow the unformed expression to emerge.

Maybe one day silence will be given the same respect that verbosity is now given.

LISTENING AND TRANS-FORMATION

Listening — a pivotal tool

It is the transformational quality of listening which gives the power to the act of consciousness-raising and breaking of taboos on certain topics. Chellis Glendinning, an American psychotherapist and peace activist, says: "In the late sixties, women in many places began to gather in small groups and tell their personal histories of life in a sexist society. In leaderless groups, women spoke with each other, telling their secrets, showing their wounds and sharing tales of childhood, puberty, marriage, birthing, birth control, work, ageing, roles and relationships. Telling these stories broke the silence and taboo, enabling women to confront their oppressive programming and figure out, as individuals and a class of people, how they could change. Telling their stories served as a basis for understanding, building community, personal transformation and political action."[3]

More recently, increased awareness of such painful issues as physical and sexual abuse, including incest and battering, addictions, and death and dying, has also come through people daring to break out of isolation and talk about these secrets, nurtured by receptive listening. Sources of hope and strength are shared, anger is mobilized, and action then follows.

There are many personal and social movements which use listening as a pivotal tool, such as the Interhelp network, Reevaluation Co-counselling communities, twelve step programs such as Alcoholics Anonymous and Alanon, Peer Support programs in schools and many other groups.

INNER LISTENING

The examples just discussed relate to listening to others; another dimension is inner listening. The same qualities of receptivity, nonjudging, alertness and curiosity apply to listening to oneself or to sources that are deeper than one's "self". This is the essence of many spiritual practices which provide a wealth of clarity, perspective and guidance for our actions in the world.

Inner listening is a time to relax the mind and body, to cultivate a sense of perspective, and to allow deeper sources of guidance and inspiration to be tapped. Some people describe this as communing with God or meditation. This inner listening can allow us to "Hear the sounds of the earth crying," as Thich Nhat Hanh, a Vietnamese Zen teacher and activist, puts it. It can provide the ground for the emergence of a larger sense of self. Our actions aimed at saving the planet then become self defence rather than altruism.[4]

John Seed, a rainforest activist of passionate intensity, described to me the way he periodically goes to the rainforest nearby, lies on the earth and covers himself with leaves to listen. John said: "I just wait and listen to the rainforest — how it might next protect itself. After a while I just know what to do next."

Activists from a diversity of backgrounds have been employing listening skills in inspiring ways.

LISTENING POSTS

Setting up formal listening posts has been used very effectively. In 1986 hundreds of women set up camp and held daily actions on the lawns of Parliament House in Canberra to draw attention to the implications of hosting US bases in Australia. The fact that it was a women's action attracted a hostile, provocative group of men, who were alcohol-fueled, waving placards and hurling abuse.

Two men who were supportive of the women's stand, Ken Golding and Graham Anderson, decided to set up a listening post which contributed to defusing this situation. With a few chairs and a simple sign "Men Willing to Listen" they set themselves up near the self-proclaimed "Men Against Dykes (M.A.D.)"camp.

Ken describes what evolved:

"I found the situation most intimidating but somehow the excitement seemed to override the fear. We set up our listening post. Several men approached us, curious at first, and initially doubting that we were there just to listen to what they had to say. It was not long before we were joined by the equally curious organizers of M.A.D. We sat and listened to their story. Derogatory references to lesbianism were continuous. They wanted to know 'why women's space?' and 'what's this got to do with peace?' There was anger as they spoke of mothers bringing children to the camp, ignoring the fact that it was men who had hurled fire bombs into the camp the night before.

"Anger and fear dominated their talk — that they, as men, were excluded, not needed, rejected. As they were allowed to talk out this anger and fear, a more pressing fear was able to surface: that this situation, which they had created, was getting out of control and lives could be in danger. There had been hundreds of men present the night before, and tonight was pay night. With a sense of urgency they left to have a 'pow-wow' which led to the M.A.D. camp breaking up."[5]

Listening posts have been used in another way by the Sydney Interhelp group. Ben Weiss, Sara Gilfillan and others set up "Peace Activists Willing to Listen" posts in Kings Cross, coinciding with the blockades of visiting US warships by the small craft of the Peace Squadron. The listening posts provided a bridge between the sailors, who sometimes felt under personal attack, members of the public wanting to express their feelings about the demonstration and those who were in favor of the demonstration.

The method was not used to try to convert anybody to another point of view but to allow people to vent frustration, anger, and strongly held opinions which led in some cases to a spontaneous softening in attitude. People were then inclined to ask questions about the wider issues at stake.

These listening posts have been inspired by Fran Peavey, who describes her adventures as a world traveler in the role of an "American Willing to Listen". She says: "But the more I studied the nuclear threat, the more I became consumed with a desire to talk with people around the world and find out how they felt about the future. I wanted to enlarge the context of my work to prevent nuclear war. Although theoretically I was fighting for the survival of every human being on the planet, I didn't actually know many people outside the United States".

Fran sat in streets in Japan, trains in India, parks in Scotland, and cafes in Thailand with a sign "American Willing to Listen". She asked, sometimes through impromptu interpreters, "Are things getting better or worse in your life? In the world?" or "What have you learned in your life?" Even when people expressed hostility towards the USA she says: "I kept listening and noticing my own defenses." Fran goes on to say:

"Since it first began four years ago my listening project has become a continuing practice — a kind of tuning up of my heart to the affairs of the world. I hear the news in a different way now and act with a larger context in mind. I hold myself accountable to the people whose lives I have seen and carry with me some of their pain. Much of my life and environment have been designed to isolate me from this pain, but I have come to see it as a kind of holy nectar. The more I drink, the more I can taste what is happening on this planet. It does not weigh me down."[6]

Door knocking has provided another vehicle for listening that has proved empowering both for the listener and the ones being listened to.

DOOR KNOCKING

Deborah Lubar, in an article "Breath", described asking residents of a suburban neighborhood simple open-ended questions, as part of a despair and empowerment workshop in Boston. After introducing herself she explained that she was taking a survey of people's concerns about the world today. :

> She asked
> 1. What do you think is the greatest problem facing the world today?
> 2. What do you consider the chances of nuclear war to be?
> 3. Do you discuss these concerns with your family, your friends, or business associates?
> 4. What do you think would make our country safe and strong?

Deborah says, "The most consistent thing I found about the answers I got, other than the greatest problem facing the world today is hunger, was that *everyone* thought the chances of nuclear war were great, and almost *no one* discussed this issue with *anyone*."[7]

She goes on to describe an extraordinarily powerful encounter with a man whose door she knocked on. Initially he responded towards her with extreme rudeness and cynicism. They just managed to keep a connection going long enough for her simple presence and interest in his feelings to lead to a surfacing of his painful nuclear nightmares. He continued to talk about his rage at his sense of powerlessness, and his longings for his children's future. She stayed with him through the grieving and raging and was able to witness a softening and unfolding of a renewed sense of hope and connection with life. She was not trying to convert him to anything but was merely present and supportive.

Not many door encounters have such depth of contact and profound intimacy, but many personal stories, dreams and fears are revealed. However, door knocking has allowed some bridging of the silence by encouraging the public to start breaking the taboos on talking about these things to each other.

For the listener, the fear of raising these topics with strangers is lessened when an open listening approach is taken. It is also illuminating to discover the depth of concern people have, and their relief at the opportunity to discuss this. It is important to have no expectations of a particular outcome, (for instance that they become active, or that they agree with your ideas.) This process is different to the other type of door knocking, where the primary purpose is fundraising.

DEMON-STRATIONS

Demonstrating — with coffee and pastries

With a willingness to listen, demonstrations can take on a less polarizing ambience. For instance, some Interhelp members — Pat Fleming and Stu Anderson among others — set up a "Cafe Anti Boom Boom" outside the French Embassy in Canberra to protest the French nuclear testing in the Pacific. Tables, chairs, coffee and French pastries were an incentive for people to join in. People were invited to write their comments on what was appreciated about the French and French culture, on a board provided, and also what was not appreciated about the way the French government was acting.

Because of the low confrontational nature of the protest, the Ambassador and some of the staff felt comfortable enough to share a bottle of French wine with the protestors. This led to a dialogue where the demonstrators could use their questioning and listening skills.

Even at the height of the civil war in Nicaragua, listening played an important role. An ongoing group of mainly US citizens formed a "Witness for Peace". They went to Nicaragua and listened to the people. By doing so, they were able to feed back to the US public accurate, moving, firsthand testimonies of the peoples' struggle against the US-backed Contras. This was a great source of strength to those US citizens who continued to work to reverse White House policies. This alternative grapevine also served to counteract the misinformation put out.

The cultivation of listening as a tool of social change is something that can deepen with time and practice. It will no doubt benefit our personal life as well as our political work, as our personal lives are, after all, essentially an expression of our politics. The power of listening may eventually prove to be a greater contribution to real social change than all the letter writing, petition signing or placard waving that is done.

EXERCISES
Listening Skills Summary
LEVEL 1 Attentive Listening
- Create a non-distracting and comfortable environment; eg. turn down the TV, offer a chair.

- Negotiate a limit on time if appropriate; eg. "Let's talk about this for 15 minutes."

- Adopt body posture that reflects your interest and involvement;
  eg. face to face
  leaning slightly forward
  interested facial expression
  maintain eye contact.

- Maintain attentive silence, unless it is appropriate to use the following:
  Short phrases that act as encouragement for the speaker to continue:
  eg. Ah hah...
   For instance...
   Then?
   Go on... I see...

ATTENTIVE LISTENING:
Do this in pairs. Partner A is invited to speak for 3–5 minutes about a personal topic (it is useful to choose one that the listener may be tempted to start discussing) while Partner B listens attentively. When Partners A have finished (the leader can signal time up) they give their partners feedback on what they noticed about their partners' level of attention. Then partners change roles and repeat the exercise.

LEVEL 2 Reflective or Active Listening
Reflective listening includes all of the skills of attentive listening plus:
- Infrequent, open-ended questions aimed at encouraging the speakers to expand or go deeper with their own theme, rather than what you as the listener want to know; eg. "How was that for you?" "How does this affect you?"

- Use short phrases which reflect your understanding of the speaker's feelings and indicate that you are listening; eg. "You look very pleased about that." "You sound like that was very frightening and confusing."

- Similarly, use short phrases that reflect your understanding of the speaker's meaning; eg. "This is a very important decision you are making." or "So the project is in jeopardy if the funds are not soon found."

- Paraphrasing — a concise response that echoes back the essence of the speaker's main message, using the same language. "What I hear you saying is that you feel you are at a major crossroad with this decision and that the prospect of a no income period and giving up your home base is a bit scary for you right now."

- Summarizing — a concise wrapping up of the major message, what decisions have been reached or which issues are still to be clarified. "So it sounds like this issue has been upsetting you for some time and contributing to your feelings of alienation from those at the center. Since we've been talking, you have decided not to take on the new project. Also you have some feedback you need to give your co-workers and you would like to do some role play preparation for this. What you haven't really stated yet is who in particular you need to say those things to."

In reflecting back your understanding of what has been said, take simple risks and be prepared to be corrected.

Reflective Listening

The purpose of this exercise is to quickly get some idea of whether you are listening fully to someone else, rather than just hearing them, and to use the opportunity to practice reflective listening. It can be a useful tool in an argument or when an argument is impending.

In pairs:

- Partner A, while holding a pen or some other object, is invited to make statements of a personal nature, such as how she or he is feeling or reacting, either now or in some particular situation; for instance: "I have trouble deciding what to do when things need doing at home and I'm not spending enough time with the kids, but the Animal Lib group is obviously needing a lot of extra help before this next big campaign."

- Partner B reflects back — by paraphrasing rather than parroting — what he or she sees as the essence of Partner A's statement; eg, "You feel torn in your loyalties."

- If you, as Partner A, are satisfied that you were really heard, both in meaning and feelings involved, (getting to the feeling of "Yes") you pass the pen to Partner B and the exercise continues in reverse. If, however, as Partner A you don't feel satisfied that Partner B is being accurate, keep holding the pen and either partner can keep restating until you get to the "Yes".

If this tool is being used with an actual conflict between two people, the partners are encouraged to make statements such as "When ... happened, I felt... and what I really want is..." rather than going into statements that attribute motives, call names or pass judgment on the other person. The partner has the right of reply only after accurately reflecting back the other person's statement.

Consider these questions either on your own or in a small group.

Planning a listening project

- **Where in your life currently do you think good quality listening could make a difference? Think about your workplace, area of social action, family and neighborhood.**
- **Who, in particular, needs an opportunity to be heard?**
- **When and how could you offer this?**
- **What sort of strategic questions are likely to get to the heart of the issue?**
- **What sort of preparation do you need?**

- **What listening stories do you have? Are there times when either you, or someone else, listened — in a way that made a significant difference to a situation?**

Your listening stories

NOTES
1. Mark Somner, "Notes on Listening", *Humpty Dumpty Report*, 1982, Interhelp Newsletter, USA.

2. Earl Koile, *Listening As A Way of Becoming*, Regency Books, Texas, USA, 1977.

3. Chellis Glendinning, "Telling Our Nuclear Stories," *Fellowship Magazine*, December, 1981. See also Chellis's book, *Waking Up In The Nuclear Age — A Book of Nuclear Therapy*, Beech Tree Books, William Morrow, N.Y., 1987.

4. See, *Thinking Like A Mountain*, Seed, Macy, Fleming & Naess, New Society Publishers, Philadelphia, 1988.

5. Ken Golding, "Winds of Change", *Interhelp News in Australia*, Autumn, 1987.

6. Fran Peavey, *Heart Politics*, New Society Publishers, Philadelphia, 1986.

7. Deborah Lubar, "Breath", *Humpty Dumpty Report*, No. 6, 1984 (*Interhelp USA Newsletter*). This story is also described in Fran Peavey's *Heart Politics*.

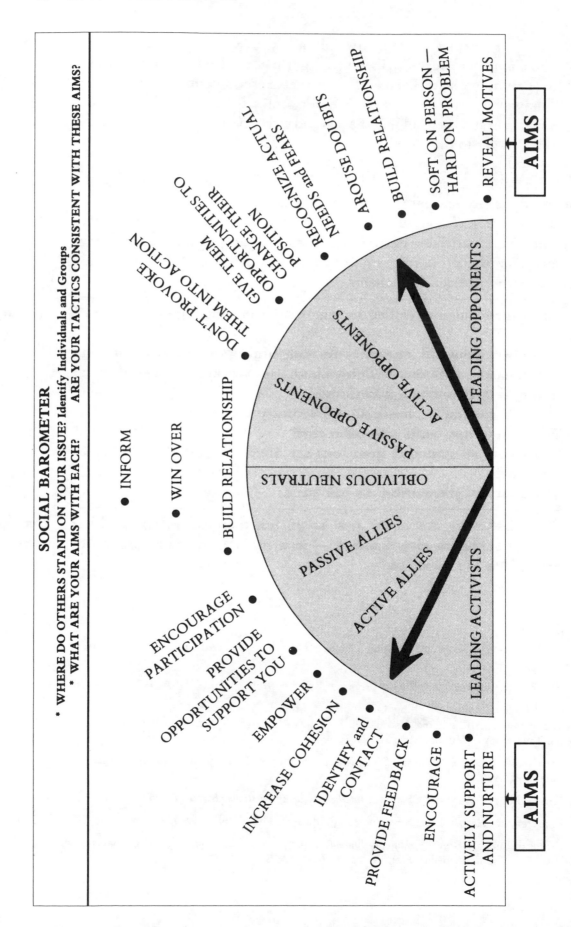

SOCIAL BAROMETER

* WHERE DO OTHERS STAND ON YOUR ISSUE? Identify Individuals and Groups
* WHAT ARE YOUR AIMS WITH EACH?   ARE YOUR TACTICS CONSISTENT WITH THESE AIMS?

AIMS

AIMS

I wish to acknowledge inspiration from David H. Albert: "People Power — Applying Non Violence Theory," New Society Publishers, Philadelphia, PA, 1985.

CHAPTER SIX
Building Bridges with the Opposition

‒‒‒

Interacting with people who have opposing views is a central task for activists committed to social change. The quality with which we approach that task has a lot to do with the effectiveness of the outcome, in both the short and long term, whether it is through lobbying, letter writing, delegations, interviews, marches or speeches.

Dealing with opposition is not, of course, just dealing with people on the so-called "other side" — the power-holders or policy makers. Often the most bitter and divisive struggles occur between factions and hard-liners on "your side".

Referring back to the social barometer (chart p 54), the key tasks for the "opponent spectrum" are to: identify who your opponents are; build relationships with them; identify their needs; arouse doubts in them; maybe expose their motives and provide them with opportunities and motivation to change their position.

The primary task when confronting the opposition — and perhaps the least obvious and the most paradoxical requirement — is to build relationships. This is a direct contradiction to the usual approach. To build relationships requires moving towards your opponents rather than away from them. You also need to be prepared to understand their point of view. This means being prepared to respectfully listen to what actually are their underlying needs and fears. In the previous chapter we discussed what a powerful effect good listening can have.

Anthea Duquemin, who has a keen interest in conflict resolution, described to me how, by really watching her reaction to opposing views, she realized how challenging it can be to listen with openness. "The first feeling I get is resistance — 'I don't want to do this'. I feel a tightening around my mind. It is as if I am trying to encapsulate my thoughts, as if I am afraid I am going to lose *my* thoughts, when I know I am going to have them challenged. If I don't have to listen, nothing has to change. What I need to do is acknowledge to myself that they have a valid view, and they are real people."

"Can the peace movement talk in loving speech, showing the way to peace? I think that will depend on whether people in the peace movement can be peace. We cannot do anything for peace without ourselves being peace." — Thich Nhat Hanh.

"What you do speaks so loudly to me that I cannot hear what you say." — Quaker saying.

> What have you observed about the way people with opposing views
> on an issue usually approach each other?
> ● What has your experience been of approaching this kind of
> conflict situation?
> ● What has your experience been of trying to persuade someone
> who has the power, to make the changes you want?
> ● What is your first reaction to contemplating being in that
> situation?

Generally we each have a characteristic response to conflict.It is
worthwhile to identify your style or recurring pattern, particularly in
dealing with authority figures. Usually power-holders will fit into that
category. (See Untangling Projection checklist p 39).

Approaching each other
like two brick walls on
legs!

As we discussed in Chapter 4, "Insight As a Resource", our emotional
reaction or interpretation may be quite distorted and exaggerated by
projection. This occurs when we attribute qualities and motives which
in fact belong to us or to figures in our past, to people we are with
now. We may become overly submissive, inappropriately rebellious, angry,
or in some other way more reactive than the situation warrants. We are
particularly prone to projecting on to authority figures — for instance,
they may "wear the face" for us of father or headteacher or some aspect
of ourselves about which we have unresolved feelings.

How often have you observed parties approach each other like two
brick walls on legs? — full of self-righteous zeal; acting as if: "with enough
airspace, the obviousness of our morally superior position will surely bring
results". In this situation people are quick to argue, cut each other off,
attribute motives, make threats and criticize. However, beneath this
approach there may be a fixed notion that actually the opposing party
are fools who are far too entrenched to ever change; if they do change
it may be seen as just another cynical ploy. It is understood that humiliation,
force or underhand tactics are OK if you end up "winning". The movement
is away from each other, by stereotyping, or even dehumanizing the
opponent. With this attitude it then becomes much easier to treat people
badly, in ways which would not normally be acceptable if they remained
"one of us". The model is derived from the world of oppositional politics
— the most dominant is set up as the most successful.

The media is eager to amplify this oppositional approach with headlines
such as "Greens Draw Battle Lines... " or "Blood Flows Over Funding
Cuts": the language of war and conflict is favored. Even good compromises
are painted in terms of defeat and humiliation, with negative reinforcement.

What are the alternatives to this all-too-familiar oppositional style? The crux of it would be to build relationships; this means adopting the "soft on the person, hard on the problem" approach, which is the basis of nonviolent philosophy and conflict resolution. To do this requires a commitment to reconciliation. Above all, it requires one to be respectful, to strive to build trust, and to be prepared to listen. One must be prepared to listen for the real needs and fears of each party, and to look for creative solutions that allow both sides to meet their needs if possible — a win/win outcome rather than a win/lose. As Gandhi said: "What kind of victory is it when someone is left defeated?"

The second aspect of the alternative approach to change is that it is important for the agent of change to learn to deal with conflict creatively and skillfuly. Like other interpersonal skills, conflict resolution skills can be learnt. Conflict is part of the very fabric of life, yet we tend to see it as a negative phenomenon. It is the major stimulus for growth on a personal and societal level and the driving, catalytic force behind changes.

BUILDING RELATION-SHIP

Apart from moral or spiritual ethics or arguments about why it is better to treat people respectfully, to do so is above all likely to be more effective. What you are doing in lobbying is selling ideas and hoping to change belief systems. These techniques are highly developed in two fields: psychotherapy and sales/marketing. As Hugh Crago points out in his article, "The Paradoxes of Change — A Psychotherapist Looks at Social Activism"[1]:

"While a positive, non-critical attitude may not be curative in and of itself, it remains the sine qua non for most successful change work with individuals and small social systems. It's so much taken for granted in my profession that its virtual absence in some other areas of change work strikes me as somewhat bizarre." This of course is equally true for all who take sales or marketing seriously. They wouldn't contemplate using the kind of approach often taken by activists — ie, behavior that is very disrespectful, argumentative or even abusive. One must question whether any thought has been given to the goal of effectiveness. Is the actual goal rather to be seen to engage in the "struggle" for its own sake?

Crago continues: " . . . as long as social change agents continue to think in terms of opponents, of evil forces to be fought, they will reach no one but the almost-converted. To say this is easy; to carry it out in practice requires a reorientation of attitudes that amounts to a revolution among revolutionaries. Hence the . . . paradox of change: We can change others only indirectly; the direct change must be to ourselves."

Nan Nicolson, a rainforest activist, describes how she finds establishing some neutral common ground a good opener for establishing a relationship:

"I remember talking to some sawmill workers about the terrible accident rates in their line of work, and the lack of compensation or even interest shown by employers or even their union. It set the tone. I had walked in as an unknown person, one of those hated ignorant greenies who were trying to destroy their jobs. By letting myself feel and express some empathy for other aspects of their situation, we had the starting point for seeing each other as real people and from there we began to talk about the issues . . . "

People who are shouted at aggressively or railroaded will automatically raise their defenses. Being listened to respectfully means having the experience of feeling heard and understood. Defenses often drop. People are then more likely to treat your response as a considered opinion, and may treat it with the same respect as you have afforded them.

Nan recalls, on another occasion, that stopping to ask a question turned a tricky situation around:

"It was at the Mt Nardi logging blockade in Northern NSW. A few of us were walking through the forest and were confronted by loggers with some mean looking doberman dogs. One of our group launched into a condescending, self-righteous sort of oratory — on why they were wrong to cut the forest. It was putting one of the loggers, particularly, into a rage, and rapidly the situation was feeling increasingly tense and potentially dangerous. It was hardly going to convince him.

"Then it occurred to me to ask the furious man for his opinion on the situation. I was so amazed by the way he quickly became reasonable and even affable. Of course it turned out he was worried about the future of his job with a young family to support. We ended up chatting about the viability of plantation timbers and reforestation schemes."

So far I have emphasized the "soft on the person" dimension that is germane to a respectful nonviolent campaign. This approach to the opposition could be dismissed as soft and naive. You may be thinking: "After all, people who are benefiting from exploiting others or the environment won't give up without being forced to"; or "If I am putting so much into making a connection, doesn't that mean I'm selling out?"; or "Will other people think I have sold out my principles?" But don't forget the other fundamental part of the formula : being "hard on the problem".

Although listening to the opposition's point of view is important it is equally important to put your position and be heard — both by the opposition and by the public. This can be quite an anxiety-provoking experience when you are not used to doing it. Something I have found useful is imaging those I represent standing behind me — whether they be environments, creatures or humans, including those of the future. They require me not to betray them by giving up my power in these situations. This has been a source of strength enabling me to speak up and not compromise.

Acting with integrity and presenting accurate, persuasive information over sufficient lengths of time will be your major tools for turning the tide of public opinion. If moral pressure on the power-holders is not sufficient, you will eventually set up conditions so it becomes expedient for them to give consumers or voters what they are now wanting. In fact, this eventually becomes essential if they want to stay in power. Therefore all your actions should be taken bearing in mind this overriding need to win over public opinion — the essential prerequisite to changing official policy. Laying the groundwork through relationship building leads to minimal polarization, which then gives the most leeway to the opposition to shift positions. Respectful campaigns also go a long way to minimize backlash.

So far I have assumed that "your side" is able to present a united front and agrees on fundamental issues. However, what is perceived as fundamentally important and possible to achieve is often an area for serious disagreement within groups and movements pushing for change. So the same spirit of reconciliation and commitment to good process will need to be applied on this level. Sometimes the hardest work is needed within your own movements or groups. (See Chapter 8 on "Working Together".)

I have described the general spirit of relationships, but what does it involve on a practical level?

PREPARATION

When facing the opposition thorough preparation makes a big difference. Make sure you have accurate facts and a lucid case — preferably written down to leave behind for later assimilation. Find out who in fact are the key people, so they emerge individually from a sea of faceless opposition. Who are the leaders, the ones with the power to make decisions? Who provides them with finance, prestige or authority? Who supports them in other ways? What sorts of statements have they made on this issue? What are their interests? Do they have significant prejudices or personal dislikes? Who in the organization is likely to be most sympathetic to your cause? What do they, as individuals and as officials, need, and how far could you help them meet their needs?

Take the time to "walk in their shoes".

As groundwork for building relationships, take the time to "walk in their shoes" — it can be very illuminating (see exercise p 65). By this I mean to step aside from your perspective and imagine yourself as this person. Try to get a real sense of how s/he experiences the world. Role playing is a potent technique for preparation. Questions and answers can be clarified and likely emotional reactions and difficulties anticipated — both yours and theirs.

I once participated in a role play preparation for a campaign to stop the establishment of a mineral sand (aggregate) processing plant. The plant would have released radioactive waste into the air and water. I took the role of the company executive who was pushing for the project to go ahead. I noticed how sure of myself I felt and how easy it was to feel that although we were going to make money — but also take financial risks — I would be doing some good for the community by establishing jobs and bringing in money to the area. There would be many people who would reinforce the idea that I was doing a good thing. I had the best resources, the best advice and lots of professional backup. I was also under pressure to make it viable, to meet deadlines and to be seen to be keeping things moving.

I got a sense of how impatient I would feel to be bothered by conservationists with vague, emotional arguments and ill-researched facts, who didn't come up to my professional way of doing things. I would also want to know exactly who they were representing and where they fitted into the hierarchical scheme of things.

PRESENTATION The way we present ourselves has a lot to do with initial reactions (which tend to last) and can have a significant impact on our acceptance, as all good sales people know. They would never jeopardize a sale by deliberately dressing inappropriately, yet this is not uncommon among activists. One said recently:

"I have had numerous arguments with people who felt that changing their dress was compromising their principles and was some sort of backdown. It's like adolescent rebellion against the folks. It's often necessary to weigh up what is more important. Needing to preserve the uniform of your group identity seems to indicate insecurity more than anything else — perhaps even arrogance."

Gandhi had enough charisma and authority to turn up in London to meet Chamberlain in a dhoti, but most of us aren't likely to pull it off successfully. It is so easy to be stereotyped and dismissed without wearing clothes or hair styles that you know are likely to get people off side. Sometimes it is as if the statement of defiance is more important than being effective.

LANGUAGE The language you use will also have a big influence on whether you meet people on the same wavelength. This refers not only to the use of particular words but also putting your case, if possible, in terms they would consider important. This is especially true in the initial rapport-building phase. Patrick Anderson relates his experience of this:

"I left India realizing that the most effective way I could work for the protection of India's forests and environment was in Australia, trying to change the sort of development assistance that funded such monstrosities as the Narada dams scheme. When I returned to Australia I made contact with the government departments responsible for handling funds to the World Bank.

"I remember entering with some trepidation the government offices, and seeing all the men in their suits and ties. The horrors of India seemed a distant dream from their air-conditioned building. The person I met was obviously annoyed that I had come to bother him with environmental concerns when clearly the real issues of the world were economic. But I persisted, and told him of the problems I had seen in the early stages of the World Bank funded dam project. I stressed that even from an economic perspective the project would be a disaster.

"Once I was able to put the problem in language that could be understood, my story was heard. The man I was dealing with started to let the information in, promised to investigate the problems I had raised and asked for more details. With persistence, lobbying and by setting up a campaign with aid and environment groups to reform Australian development aid, things have changed. The government departments responsible for administering the aid now take environmental concerns seriously and are starting to play a significant role in changing the environment policy of the World Bank."

I have observed Patrick on many occasions applying his skills of nonviolent communication. He is non-blaming, stresses the positive side and areas of agreement, and doesn't attribute motives to people's actions. It certainly works to disarm and engage people who could easily become very oppositional.

All this doesn't imply that we need to become only mild-mannered, receptive listeners; or, given the dominant paradigm, that we only phrase things in economic terms. There is of course a place for impassioned, emotional pleas from the heart — at the right moment they will dissolve a wall of rationalist arguments, but it does require a lot of clarity and sensitive observation to discern the moment when such oratory will have impact.

NEGOTIATION

Negotiation is an art in itself with clearly defined skills that can be learned and applied. It is not my purpose to outline them here, but to give

Looking for the win/ win solution

encouragement to seek out some of the excellent resources for developing these skills. (See suggested reading.) Having at least some basic knowledge in this area can prove to be an ever-useful contribution to social change movements, for bringing about reconciliation in all sections of the social spectrum.

Is a win/win solution possible? For example, is it possible for the company to continue to make reasonable profits but not to make environmentally unsound products or exploit workers in the process? It may mean creating face-saving options or strategies. Face-saving is perceived negatively in our culture, yet in many others it is given high priority. It will make it much more likely that people who back off a publicly stated position with their image intact will not lust for opportunities for revenge, or wait for an opportunity to undermine the changes.

I believe there is wide scope for skilled negotiators who are not allied with lobby groups (and who can present themselves as objective) to act as intermediaries in these sorts of conflicts eg. environmental mediators. Also setting up such specialized services within communities is a valuable contribution to bridge building.

NON-VIOLENT ACTION

There will be many issues where lobbying, no matter how skilfully it is done, will not bring about the needed changes. This spirit of "hard on the problem, soft on the people" can pervade the other tactics such as civil disobedience or direct actions which may include blockades, boycotts, sit ins, vigils or mass rallies, marches or demonstrations. (Gene Sharp compiled a list of 198 nonviolent tactics to choose from.[2])

The philosophy and practice of nonviolent action requires more than abstinence from violence, and more than well thought out strategies and tactics; it requires an inner commitment and consistency of integrity, whatever the reaction of the opponent. Nonviolent campaigns have a strong proven record throughout history — a record which is nearly obscured by the glorification of violence and war.

Martin Luther King said, "I do not want to give the impression that nonviolence will work miracles overnight. People are not easily moved from their mental ruts or purged of their prejudice and irrational feelings. When the underprivileged demand freedom, the privileged first react with bitterness and resistance. Even when the demands are couched in nonviolent terms, the initial response is the same, so the nonviolent approach does not immediately change the heart of the oppressor. It first does something to the hearts and souls of those committed to it. It gives them a new self respect; it calls up resources of strength and courage they didn't know they had. Finally it reaches the opponent and so stirs his conscience that reconciliation becomes a reality."[3]

You never know when unexpected allies are going to show up from where you least expect them. Robert Hunter in a thrilling book, "*The Greenpeace Chronicle*"[4], describes how on their way to protest the nuclear testing by the US Government at Amchitka the Greenpeace boat was boarded and the crew arrested by a US Coast Guard vessel. A cablegram arrived which said:

"Due to the situation we are in, the crew of the '*Confidence*' feel that what you are doing is for the good of all mankind. If our hands were not tied by these military bonds, we would be in the same position you are in if it were at all possible. Good luck! We are behind you one hundred per cent."

A petition was also signed by many of the crew members of the coast guard, supporting their stand. Later Hunter says, " For the crew of a US Coast Guard ship to have signed a petition supporting a foreign vessel leading an attack on their own government was tantamount to treason. It laid them open to all sorts of penalties, maybe even court martial. It was a high, intense moment, enough to bring me to the edge of tears." Gifts and souvenirs were surreptitiously exchanged and when the men left, the gifts created absurd little bulges in their wetsuits.

What you are being *rather than* doing *has the greatest influence.*

The sequel was that some of the crew of the '*Confidence*' were fined and some junior officers demoted. However, all the other coast guard "volunteers" who were doing nothing more than avoiding being sent to Vietnam, had refused to take over the positions of the demoted officers, with the result that the officers were reinstated. The fines were paid for by a supportive group, so the crew had escaped the consequences of the mutiny without a scratch.

Ultimately it is what you are *being* rather than *doing* individually and collectively that has the greatest influence. This quality of being requires becoming conscious of patterns and habitual responses. It means knowing you have a choice to adopt more effective ways and learn new skills.

"I had always had a bit of a thing about policemen, especially after so many confrontations at direct actions," says Nan Nicolson. "However recently I had an experience which really shook my stereotyping around. Much to my surprise I was approached by a cop for a job reference, even though we had only met a few times. He apparently needed someone from a minority group, even a member of the 'lunatic fringe', to say he was a reasonable man and would listen to others' viewpoints.

"My initial reaction was 'Why should I?'; then came my learned reaction of 'Yeah, give it a go, something useful will probably come out of it'. I must admit my decision was compounded by the thought that it wouldn't be a bad thing to have a cop indebted to me.

"So I wrote the reference and was surprised to get a letter from him soon after in which he thanked me, and went on at length to reveal his passionate feelings about the danger the planet was in, the way development would kill us all. He had not told me any of this beforehand as he did not want to prejudice the reference by appearing to have similar views. Of course I was pleased I had helped him. I learnt a lot from that encounter, and now consider him an ally."

EXERCISES

Grounding Preparation for Confrontation

The notion of being grounded implies being "down to earth", alert, aware of emotions but not thrown off balance by them. The purpose of this exercise is to give yourself a bodily sense of calm, groundedness and determination. This may be useful in a situation where you feel anxiety or know you are likely to give way under pressure.

Have someone read the instructions to you or put them on tape to play to yourself. This exercise can be done in a sitting position (with spine upright) if needed.

Stand with your feet slightly apart and knees very slightly bent. Close your eyes, or allow your gaze to become soft and unfocussed. Relax, slow down your breathing, and put particular emphasis on a slower outbreath. Continue this for several breaths . . .

Now let your abdomen relax . . . dropping your shoulders and letting your chest open, more and more as you breathe. Keep doing this for a few minutes till you feel calmer . . .

Become aware of the soles of your feet . . . aware of the sensation of contact with the ground . . . imagine yourself growing roots down

into the earth from the soles of your feet... deep down into the earth... imagine these roots drawing strength from the earth... now let that sense of strength travel right up your spine... Be aware of your backbone, feel its strength and also its flexibility...

Now think of those people you are representing here whom you care for; think of their faces, names... perhaps also beings of the future generations... and now bring to mind any other creatures, forms of life or even places that you might also represent in this situation... feel the presence of all of these standing firmly behind you, lending strength and conviction to what you need to express... Be aware that you may be their only advocate in this situation...

Take some final deep breaths... open your eyes and keep that feeling in your body... slowly start to move... Now you are ready to face what comes from a calm and strong position.

If you start to lose this feeling during your interactions or just before giving your talk, you can unobtrusively switch your attention to your breathing or the sense of roots beneath your feet, or to sensing the presence of those you are representing. The ability to do this will improve the more times you practice this exercise.

Walking in their Shoes

This exercise is designed to develop empathy with and understanding of people you need to build a relationship with, and who have differing perspectives from yours. This empathy will enable you to respond more appropriately and have more realistic expectations and, it will provide the basis for ongoing dialogue despite differences.

To do the exercise, either have someone read the questions to you or else after reading each question yourself, close your eyes for a couple of minutes while you formulate your response. The important thing is to allow yourself to *be* that person as much as possible, such as actors do when immersing themselves into roles.

"To walk a mile in their shoes first you need to remove your own."

Select a particular person whom you are going to have to confront or persuade. If there is no one specifically known to you, let yourself imagine what he or she might be like. If known to you, try adopting that person's body posture, mannerisms and voice when you answer. Now being this person, respond to these questions (do it out loud if you wish):

● **What is your position and what are your responsibilities? How did you come to be there?**

- **What is your life like? What really matters to you?**

- **What is your perspective on the issue in question?**

- **What are you afraid might happen?**

- **What pressures and expectations are operating in your life?**

- **How are you likely to perceive this lobby group or person who wants to influence you?**

- **What are the constraints on your cooperating with them?**

Now just breathe quietly for a couple of minutes and reflect on what important clues you may have learnt about this person from this exercise. What will help you approach the person constructively? What attitude and form of questioning will be helpful in gaining respect and cooperation?

It is important to derole and debrief afterwards. Do this by concentrating on stepping back into your own shoes. Discuss with your partner who read out the questions what you discovered from doing this exercise.

It is helpful to redo this exercise when more is known after subsequent meetings.

Mapping Conflict[5] Mapping conflict is an extremely useful tool that can be applied in a great range of conflict situations. It is especially useful when there is confusion, with seemingly a lot of factors involved or when it is hard to understand why people are behaving the way they are. Creating a map tends to clarify the picture quickly. It can be done alone — in which case you guess the other party's needs and fears — but it is best to do it with those with whom you are in conflict. Use a large sheet of paper or wall board.

STEP 1 Define the issue of contention with a short, neutral title. Write this in the middle of the map.
STEP 2 Identify the major parties in the conflict. They may be individuals or groups (they can be lumped together if they share the same needs) You may find a combination of individuals and groups. Draw a section on the map for each party.
STEP 3 List all the significant NEEDS (this includes what is most valued,

RESIDENTS WHO SUPPORT TAVERN	DEVELOPERS
NEEDS • Social drinking venue • Bring money/jobs into village *FEARS* • Don't want other group to increase power (thin end of wedge.) • Opening up of community divisions.	*NEEDS* • Increased income • Return on investment so far • Maintain goodwill in community *FEARS* • Lose money on unrealized investment • Being dictated to by "trouble makers".

PROPOSED TAVERN IN THE VILLAGE

RESIDENTS WHO OPPOSE TAVERN	IMMEDIATE NEIGHBORS
NEEDS • To have say in local development which will affect them. • Maintain unique character of village. • A community facility especially for children and adolescents. *FEARS* • Teenage drinkers • Drink-drivers on roads • Safety in village • Change social character of village.	*NEEDS* • Maintain neighborly relationships • Maintain quality of immediate home environment (peace & quiet). *FEARS* • Open up community divisions • Unruly behavior • Decreased esthetics • Decreased property values • Pollution of creek — sewerage.

and what you/they care about). Ask yourself: "With this issue of . . . what are my/our/their most important needs?

STEP 4 Repeat this listing for each party, asking: "What are the significant fears/concerns/worries?" Don't dismiss them even if they are irrational — they are still likely to be motivating players.

Check whether there are fears linked to needs or vice versa (implied but not stated).

Resist the temptation to get going prematurely on solutions, but rather stay focussed on the mapping until it is complete. If other issues or conflicts become apparent that are not part of this issue, note them for later mapping and return to the initial focus. If necessary, put yourself in the place of those not present. (See walking in their shoes exercise p 65). What would they say are their needs and fears?

When the map is complete:
- Peruse it for new insights.
- Would it be useful to break the problem down into smaller parts?
- Highlight areas on which you need more information.
- Look for areas of common ground and common vision on which to build win/win solutions.
- Look for areas which need particular attention or emphasis in the forming of possible solutions.

From this map you can move on to generating lists of options for possible solutions that meet the needs and address the fears of the parties. It is also worth considering what the alternatives or consequences are if agreement cannot be reached.

The next stage is to evaluate and negotiate the options to find one which is most suitable and mutually acceptable. Formulating a plan of action to implement solutions is the next step. It is often useful to suggest trying something out for a set period of time and arrange review processes to discuss whether more changes need to be made.[5]

NOTES
1. Hugh Crago, "The Paradoxes of Change", *Australian Society Magazine*, December, 1984.

2. Martin Jelfs (Revised by Sandy Merritt), *Manual For Action*, Action Resources Group, London, 1982.

3. Quoted in Ram Dass & Paul Gorman, *How Can I Help*? Alfred A. Knopf, New York, 1986.

4. Robert Hunter, *The Green Peace Chronicle*, Picador, Pan Books, London, 1980.

5. I learned this from the Conflict Resolution Network. For a fuller explanation, see Cornelius and Faire, *Everybody Can Win*, Simon & Schuster, Sydney, 1989.

CHAPTER SEVEN

Presenting the Bad News

To be aware and active on social issues brings us face to face with a lot of bad news — whether it is on the state of the environment, how wide-spread corruption and organized crime is, the incidence of sexual assault, human rights or whatever else we choose to focus on from the litany of 20th Century horrors. We do need this accurate information to be able to take appropriate action. We also need to inform others. Presenting potentially distressing information — whether by giving a talk, slide show, film or even by a magazine article — can be handled in such a way as to allow the audience to integrate or digest the information emotionally as well as intellectually.

It is also desirable to leave the audience with an ability to respond and a feeling of connection with others who share similar concerns, rather than leaving them feeling overwhelmed and hopeless.

The following suggestions are integral to good education. These principles often are forgotten amidst the pressures of urgency or seriousness. Before all else, think of yourself as a facilitator rather than a lecturer or expert. If you are used to being "the expert lecturer" some courage and flexibility is required to give up being the center of attention, the one in control. This will foster participation.

Ask yourself: Are you angry with "the public" for not doing enough on this particular issue?

Start by asking yourself about your feelings and motivations for presenting the information in the first place. Are you angry with "the public" for not doing enough on this particular issue? Is it possible you would prefer to leave your audience feeling a bit guilty? Are you primarily intending to raise funds rather than have more people get actively involved in your group? Do you currently feel hopeless — that nothing can actually be done? Is it really essential that they get all the facts today?

In most cases you will get a better response from presenting some facts, structuring in some digestion time and exercises, yet leaving the group still fresh enough to begin to act in at least some small way. If you provide leads, they can later find out more if they wish.

Audiences will rarely complain if you talk at them for an hour; we are conditioned by schooling and entertainment to silently consume information. However, if you are boring or overwhelming them by too much distressing information, they may just silently tune out. The signs of this happening are glazed eyes, yawning, and chair shifting. Some may even slink silently off, perhaps feeling depressed and isolated. Watching the body language of the group will give you good cues as to what is appropriate.

The facilitator is likely to be more excited and wide awake than the audience — worrying about what comes next, or perhaps engrossed in audio-visual equipment. The upshot is often failure to stay tuned to the group as a whole. One way around this is to arrange others to be in the audience as "vibes watchers". Ask these people to gauge the general mood of the group, and to either stand up and suggest a break or an activity, or else send a signal to the facilitator to switch modes.

"Vibes watchers" gauge the group's moods.

The general principles presented below could apply to many different situations: for instance, an educational talk on AIDS, a slide show on the destruction of tropical rainforests, an anti-nuclear film, or a public meeting on local crime. In these examples the discussion is more formal, in contrast to workshops where there would be more scope and safety for dealing with deeper feelings.

GENERAL PRINCIPLES

INTEGRATION & EMPOWERMENT

1. *Pitch the presentation appropriately.*
In the preparatory stage, before the actual presentation, give some thought to who your audience is and put yourself "in their shoes". What are their values? What style will allow them to feel comfortable? How does this issue relate to their lives? Are they used to talking about their feelings? Would they have ever been given an opportunity? Have they chosen to attend this presentation or is it compulsory, part of an overall program?

2. *Warm-up is important.*
The first few minutes particularly will influence what sort of responses you get; hence you can help your audience by warming them up to sharing and involvement. Welcome the audience and thank them for expressing their concern on this issue by turning up. You can set the tone by sharing a little of yourself — your personal link with the issue. "I first became aware of this problem when ..." or "Whenever I give this talk I feel ..." Let your passions show in order to infuse the facts with a more human quality.

Sometimes it is important to acknowledge that the material can be hard to face or that it could be distressing. Validate people's feelings and questions. Create an atmosphere of "we are all in this together, and by working together we can find solutions".

3. *Don't overload people with too much information.*

Particularly if the information is disturbing. Giving more and more information in itself does not activate people — at some level we are already aware that our planet is in deep trouble. As was suggested in Section 1, we need opportunities to integrate factual material with the totality of our beings, and to deal with the anguish that arises when we take in the implications of the material. Give enough information to provide an overview; details could be provided in handouts.

4. *Involve the audience.*

This is probably the most important principle. Involvement will maintain attention, assist in integrating more deeply what is presented, and lessen isolation. We all need to form relationships with others who share our concerns, and to know that our contributions make a difference. Involvement is enhanced by introducing people to each other, finding out what they really wish to know, and providing opportunities for processing thoughts and feelings together.

First consider how the chairs are arranged. For instance, a semi-circle around a speaker rather than straight rows will create a more informal atmosphere and allow people to see each other. Further suggestions on involvement are given below and in Chapter 14.

5. *Provide Hope.*

Rather than battering the audience with terrifying information and graphic details of negative scenarios, it is important to leave people with some sense of hope. For instance, emphasizing that the threat of nuclear weapons is a human issue, and not just a technological one, implies that it is ordinary people who can be the ones to make a difference. Though the power holders will end up taking the credit for changes in policy, they are basically responding to shifts in public opinion. It is empowering to highlight the fact that people don't need to be experts to respond and to get involved.

It really helps to give examples of things that ordinary people have done that made a difference — personal illustrations that give glimpses of what is possible. It is also useful to give a perspective on what achievements your particular movement has made so far.

6. *Provide information on how people could take action.*

Prepare handouts to take home with information about local resources, contacts, groups and suggestions for actions the audience could take, including sample letters they could write. Having these to take home increases the likelihood that they will follow on with action or involvement after your presentation. Encourage creative responses.

7. *Watch out for people needing extra support.* Link them up with someone who can spend some time listening to them. At the end of the presentation you could make the suggestion that individuals who feel particularly moved

by the issue, spend some time writing, drawing or talking with a supportive person to further integrate the material if they feel the need.

TECHNIQUES FOR INVOLVING THE AUDIENCE

In the introductory phase, if the group is small enough, ask them why they came and what they would like to learn. This could be done as a brainstorm, a "go around", where each person in turn is invited to make a brief statement, or at random. When someone makes a comment you could ask: "Who else has felt like this?" or "Who else came for this reason?" or "Who came for a different reason? " Then invite them to add a little more. In larger groups you could suggest: "Turn to a person near you, share a little about yourself and why you came." A show of hands is another way, i.e. "Who came tonight because ... ? " or "Who was curious about ... ?". Then weave the presentation around the concerns that were expressed.

Intersperse cognitive or heady material with the experiential mode. Experiential exercises can be initially threatening to those unfamiliar with them. However it is surprising what people are willing to do when a suggestion is skilfully presented.

It is surprising what people are willing to do when a suggestion is skilfully presented.

Margaret White, a Perth psychotherapist and business consultant, induced a group of Asian businessmen attending a business related seminar to do an exercise that involved playing with plasticine on the floor. They became so totally engrossed that they didn't want to stop.

Introduce activities in a matter-of-fact way and provide a rationale for doing so. For instance, "We know that information can often be easier to take in when we allow some time to reflect on it in a different way". Simple exercises, such as taking turns in pairs to complete open sentences, can give individuals the opportunity to share thoughts and feelings. An example is: "What comes to mind when I hear this material is ..." or "The scene/information that had the most impact on me is..." A series of questions that I have used many times is from Joanna Macy's *Despair and Personal Power in the Nuclear Age*[1]. (See exercise "Open Sentences on Our Concerns" at the end of this chapter.)

Short guided visualizations may be appropriate as a pleasant break from listening to the presentation. These can be aimed at enhancing the message you are trying to convey, such as: imaging being a rainforest that has existed for eons and is home to 10 million species. Visualizations could also be aimed at envisioning creative problem-solving, such as: suggesting they step into the future, whereupon they tell a child about the way nuclear weapons were dismantled; or how white Australians came to live in harmony and equality with Aboriginal Australians.

Give the group permission to let you know when they are starting to drift or feel overloaded. A short "buzz" break (talking amongst themselves) will revive their ability to continue. Sometimes it may be appropriate to include songs or a light-hearted game to revive and connect people.

Brainstorms can be effective to get people actively contributing, either in the whole group or in smaller groups. They are also useful for generating quickly a lot of ideas or options. (See suggested topics in the exercise, "Brainstorming" at the end of this chapter.)

Consider using stories, parables and myths to enliven the factual material. Or invite the audience, in small groups, to create parables that illustrate their perception of the situation.

Invite people to share their personal stories — of how this issue has touched their lives or what their personal contribution towards it has been. Sharing these stories will often add depth and power to an otherwise objective treatment of the issue.

A. TALKS provide great flexibility in that you can respond to the needs of the audience by continually readjusting your presentation. A rule of thumb might be to spend about 50 per cent of your time presenting facts and the rest of the time on integration and empowerment exercises and feedback. Don't make the overall presentation too long.

SOME SPECIFIC SUGGESTIONS FOR DIFFERENT MEDIUMS

B. SLIDE SHOWS. Extra visual images create a lot of impact. You can consider interspersing negative images with some positive ones, e.g. a successful reafforestation project if your talk was on forestry issues. Though it is harder to be aware of the audience engagement with the lights dimmed, stopping in the middle of a series of slides to allow some discussion may enable people to stay open to the rest of the show.

C. FILMS or VIDEOS can have great impact. Announce business before the film. Do some exercises which help people to get to know each other. Give any planned speech before the film rather than after. Let people know they will have an opportunity to talk after the film; a larger group could be divided into smaller groups beforehand. If a video is particularly disturbing, you can put it on pause and encourage talking; there is no point in continuing if people have gone numb. Don't stand up after the film and present even more horrifying facts.[2]

Don't forget that there are a lot of other creative modes for presenting information and activating people. The "Atomic Comics" in the USA and the "Bombshells", and "Circus Oz" in Australia use humor to emphasize the absurdity of the arms race and other issues. Laughter is very healing and assists us to unnumb ourselves about frightening things. You don't need to be a professional comedian — use your own sick jokes if necessary!

Laughter is very healing.

Songs, poetry, art and cartoon backdrops have been used to dramatic effect and can be scattered through a factual presentation. They can be just as effective as any serious information in raising our consciousness on issues, and in prompting us to respond.

As we will see in Section 3 — "Preventing Burnout" — it is important to make a concerted commitment to look after yourself, particularly if you are continuing to research and present disturbing material. Also be aware of the stress involved in being a facilitator. As we discussed in Section 1, despair and empowerment work can provide an emotional cleansing and lead to renewal of energy. It helps to do this work as part of a group or with a partner. This allows ongoing support, debriefing and feedback. Refer to Chapter 10 on activists' support groups, for ideas on how these groups can work.

Patrick Anderson, Director of rainforest campaigns for Greenpeace in Europe, describes how he realized the importance of these principles in his work:

"I remember a talk I gave in India, a couple of years ago. I had been in the country for five months. From north to south, I had witnessed, through the eyes of my hosts and contacts, India's environment being laid waste by industrial development. Despite all of the strong-spirited people I met who were working to turn that tide, and the many successes that they have had, my heart was filled with despair and outrage at what I had seen.

"This was to be my last talk in India before returning to Australia. The audience was made up of local activists, state politicians and press. On the verge of my departure, I felt full of desperate need to communicate to these people the extent of the destruction of nature I had witnessed throughout India. I wanted to convey the need for strong concerted action to stop the desecration of nature and culture.

"My audience was attentive and listened well. I found the eyes of one person that gave me strength and connection to speak. But my passion was too strong. My talk dealt excessively with the devastation I had seen. I had switched on to automatic, fired by my grief — detailing all the horror.

"I caught the eyes of my 'friend' again and saw that they had gone glassy. I looked at my watch and saw that most of the hour had gone. I stopped, took a breath and described the feelings inside that had driven me to talk without listening. The audience took a breath too, and I went on briefly to outline positive developments I had seen, and ways we could work together on these issues, before finishing with ten minutes of questions.

"After the talk I spoke with the young journalist who had held my eyes during the talk. I apologised for losing touch with the audience and said how much I had learnt through the talk. She said everyone in her position is aware of the environmental problems, but few can see a way out of the tangle of power and greed that is perpetuating the problem.

"I realized most of my talk had dealt with information that these people didn't need. The information that was useful to them, examples of successful campaigns, of how other people had dealt with problems in similar situations, had been squeezed into the last ten minutes."

Balancing facts with emotional integration is very important.

So these principles of an empowerment approach illustrate that although we will need to continue sharing bad news with each other, we can come away feeling motivated, inspired by whatever good news there is and in touch with other people. Balancing facts with emotional integration is important and it can be done lovingly and skilfully.

EXERCISES

- What are your motives for giving this presentation?

- Whom are you addressing? What is likely to be their perspective on life and on this issue in particular? What approach/language/environment will be most likely to get through to them?

Preparation Checklist

- What are the 3 major points you wish people to remember after this presentation?

- What sort of atmosphere will your presentation and venue create? Is it likely to be comfortable and welcoming?

- How are you intending to encourage participation and help people digest the information you offer?

- What else can you do that will contribute towards the empowerment of your audience?

- How can you make the occasion as multisensory as possible? Have you considered including music, comedy or some activity to keep concentration up?

- What are you offering in the way of follow-up to your presentation? Can you suggest people meet as working or support groups afterwards?

- Is it feasible to do a rehearsal? (Videoing your presentation will give you a tool for refining it.) Who could give you useful feedback?

- What do you as organizers or presenters need to do to look after yourselves during this project?

- Have you double checked the equipment — to see that it works well and you know how to use it?

Open Sentences on our Concerns

The following open sentences, adapted from Joanna Macy's material[3], tap concerns about the environment but could be modified to other issues. Often people have never spoken to anyone before about what they feel, and if they have they may have felt they had to justify their position. The exercise is done in pairs, with the listening partner asked to just listen respectfully and not respond. The facilitator either reads the sentences out to the whole group, one at a time, pausing for 2–3 minutes for the reply, or writes them on cards or on a board where everyone can see them. (It takes approximately 20 minutes per partner.)

1. I think the condition of our environment is becoming...

2. When I think of the world we are going to leave for our children, it looks like...

3. One of my worst fears for the future is...

4. The feelings I carry around with me about all this are...

5. When I try to share these feelings with other people, what usually happens is...

6. The ways I avoid expressing these feelings are...

7. The ways I can help other people deal with their feeling of pain for our world are...

8. What gives me hope, strength or courage is...

Another series of questions adapted from the same source is very useful for focussing attention on people's goals and resources. It would be a suitable end to a session. Participants work in pairs, taking turns. In response to questions from the facilitator, one speaks while the other records his or her answers with pen and paper; they then reverse roles. The questions are:

Identifying Goals and Resources

1. If you were totally fearless, and in possession of all your powers, what would you do to heal our world (or do about this problem that the presentation has been dealing with?) Note: encourage people to be bold but also realistic.

2. What strengths and resources do you now have that would help you do that?

3. What would you need to learn or acquire?

4. What obstacles are you likely to put in the way of fulfilling this goal?

5. What can you do in the next 24 hours — no matter how small the step — that will help you reach that goal?

A brainstorm is created by inviting a group to call out ideas at random on a topic. The ideas offered are written up as short phrases, in large letters, where everyone can see them. No discussion or debate is entered into while the storming is going on. Stress that there are no right or wrong answers or that contradictory suggestions may get put up. Brainstorming can be followed by a discussion of the ideas.

Brainstorming

Some of the following topics may be relevant:

● POPULAR MISCONCEPTIONS ON THIS TOPIC ARE...

● THINGS IN MY DAILY LIFE THAT HOLD ME BACK FROM ACTING ARE...

● WHAT CAN ONE PERSON DO...?

● WHAT COULD MY GROUP/FAMILY/NEIGHBORHOOD DO...?

● WHAT GIVES ME HOPE...?

Checklist for Debriefing after your Presentation
- How in tune with your audience did you feel as you gave the presentation?
- When did the audience seem most engaged; when were they least engaged? What made the difference?
- How do you think people were left feeling, on the whole, after the presentation? What feedback did you get?
- What did you learn from this experience?
- What changes and improvements would you make next time?
- How are you feeling after this? Are you numbing yourself in any way against the feelings that this issue raises for you?
- What do you need to do to take care of yourself and leave the issue aside for the moment? For instance, do you need to talk it over, go for a walk or take a warm bath?

NOTES

1. Joanna Macy, *Despair and Personal Power in the Nuclear Age*, New Society Publishers, Philadelphia, USA, 1983, p 96.

2. I have drawn inspiration for this section from Fran Peavey's article "Showing Anti-Nuclear Films" in Joanna Macy's *Despair and Personal Power in the Nuclear Age*.

3. Joanna Macy, *ibid*.

CHAPTER EIGHT
Working Together

T he following two chapters are not intended to be a comprehensive coverage of these topics (which are well covered elsewhere — see Suggested Reading). Rather they represent what in my observations are key issues for community-based action groups.

How many times has your involvment in groups been more of a struggle than a joy? How often has your organization failed to achieve what you so passionately seem to want? Good intentions don't seem to be enough when it comes to working together well to achieve social change goals.

What qualities would your ideal working group have? Perhaps qualities like enjoyment, mutual respect, non-exploitative relationships, getting the job done efficiently, clarity about what's happening and why. How close is this to the reality of your group or groups to which you have belonged? What do you think it would take to create this situation?

One way of looking at how we run groups (and create our communities for social change) is to think in terms of the "Holographic Paradigm"[2]. A holograph is an image which reflects, in each minute part, the image of the whole. This means making our groups and organizations function the way we would want the world to be. Imagine if each aspect of how we approach what we do together reflected what we are wishing to create. Means are consistent with the ends. For instance, if as a peace group you are wanting to decrease conflict in the world, it requires paying close attention to conflict resolution in the group, and thereby reaching deeper understandings about the roots of conflict.

> I once worked at a health center where stress-related illness and burnout was common, morale was low and some workers felt exploited by low wages and excessive demands. The challenge was to take stock of what messages we were giving clients and showing, by example, responsibility for self care and health.

"Central to the advancement of human civilization is the spirit of open enquiry. We must learn not only to tolerate our differences. We must welcome them as the richness and diversity which can lead to true intelligence." — Albert Einstein.

"What is different about living in the nuclear age is that the principle of reciprocity can no longer be viewed as an abstract ideal, but as a pragmatic method for achieving our long-term survival and security." — Lapid and Schindler. [1]

"The means are to the ends as the seed is to the tree." — Ghandi.

How can we build-in personal empowerment, at every level, in our groups?

Feelings of powerlessness are very pervasive in our society. They are the ever-present boogie that we all face in different ways, when responding to social and ecological problems of this magnitude. Each long term goal has the potential to feel like the impossible. Burnout and inner fragmentation are also common problems. These flow from the individual to become group problems such as wingeing, disharmony in relationships, fragmentation or ineffectiveness in getting the job done; therefore the way we go about working together should take this into account.

CREATING EMPOWERING GROUPS

There are two dimensions that need to be strong and balanced for a group to be effective and empowering. The first is clarity and efficiency in completing the tasks that are achieving your central purpose. This could be called the content or task dimension. The second dimension is concerned with building and maintaining good relationships. This could be called the maintenance process or people dimension.

Have you ever been part of an action group that had a good purpose, but faded out because people couldn't stand to be part of it any more?

Loose, community-based, voluntary and semi-voluntary groups are not easy to run well. It requires dedication to create the situation in which these two dimensions are well developed and in balance. As anyone who has experienced both the business world and community grass roots groups knows, it is often easier to maintain this balance in more structured organizations.

Activist groups often tend to put more value on the task dimension, until the neglected relationship side forces its way onto the agenda or the group disintegrates.

QUALITIES OF A WELL-FUNCTIONING GROUP

Affirmation is a powerful motivator.

What qualities have you noticed in groups that do empower their members?

The following list is from my observations about what makes a difference:

1. *Belonging and Valuing* — Let people know they do belong and that their contributions are valued. One aspect of this is welcoming and fully orienting new members. Create a positive atmosphere in which people feel affirmed, in which positive strokes are given easily and often. Affirmation is a powerful motivator — yet the more common practice is not to give feedback to each other or to mention only negative things.

2. *Being Clear About the Task* — When consistent attention is given to planning, policies, procedures and roles, it is clear what needs to be done, why, by whom and when. Lack of clarity in this area is a major source

of disempowerment in small community groups. (See Chapter 12, on planning.)

3. *Creating Safety* — It helps if members think about each other and give each other encouragement to keep developing inner resources, build confidence, overcome limitations and express feelings. In this environment feelings are not swept aside as irrelevant, irrespective of whether they are about the issue or about other people in the group.

4. *Listening and Consulting* — Groups in which people are listened to and consulted about things that affect them, share power and foster participation. Though at times it may be appropriate to have strong and directive leadership, this does not exclude proper listening and consultation and it does include paying attention to integrity in decision-making processes.

5. *Respecting Diversity and Uniqueness* — In voluntary community based groups especially, it is recognized as appropriate to have different rhythms, time commitments and working styles. As far as possible, people are encouraged to find the thing they love to do and can uniquely offer. Different cultural, racial, age or class backgrounds and life perspectives are valued and respected.

6. *Being Aware of Oppression* — Recognize that we are rooted in the structures that we seek to change and therefore the same problems are likely to surface in the microcosm of the group. Sexism, racism, classism and ageism will be ever present in the group, reflecting the values of society. This can shift when members are both confronted and supported to change oppressive attitudes and patterns. Policies of affirmative action help counteract structural bias.

7. *Being Committed to Conflict Resolution* — Groups that see conflict as an opportunity for development rather than as something that is bad and to be avoided, are more likely to flourish. Maintaining this attitude means being prepared to give feedback and stay with difficulties till they are resolved. Making this commitment enables far deeper levels of cohesion and satisfaction to be reached than in groups that gloss over conflict.

8. *Encouraging and Supporting Leadership* — Each person in the group is treated as a potential leader and the role of leadership is shared and demystified. (See Chapter 9.)

Often the best work happens when people are also having a good time!

9. *Training and Developing Skills* — People are encouraged to identify areas

for development to enable them to improve what they do. This could include preparation for nonviolent action, typing, book-keeping, conflict resolution, meeting facilitation or burnout prevention strategies.

10. *Sharing Visions and Encouraging Each Other's Dreams* — Taking the time to look together at common visions will enhance creativity and motivation.

11. *Making Room for Fun and Humour* — How great it is to be with people for whom working does not exclude playing! Often the best work happens when people are also having a good time!

(See the rating scale, p 164, as a tool for assessing how you would rate your group on each of these factors.)

It doesn't seem to "just happen" that a group has an atmosphere where these qualities are developed. It does take quite a lot of experimentation with good tools, as well as patience and persistence, to keep the group moving in a positive direction.

On the task dimension, it may require finding appropriate management and decision-making structures, or using project management tools, including step-by-step planning. In the dimensions of relationships, it is vital to develop cooperative processes and techniques for communication, and find satisfying meeting procedures and decision-making tools.

There are many tools available from sources such as nonviolent action training,[3] (particularly the work done by the Movement for a New Society[4]), the women's movement, business and organizational psychology. (See Suggested Reading.) We can also learn a lot from other cultures, particularly tribal societies, that will help us unlearn the competitive, oppressive or just plain unskilful ways that our culture often fosters.

THE TYRANNY OF STRUCTURELESSNESS

Sometimes, unfortunately, getting self-conscious about group process activates the rebellious side of some members' personalities. Some may be fueled by anger and passion to get on with campaigning. For some people structure may remind them of hierarchical situations, school or other places that they found oppressive or restrictive; or it may be a case of situations that failed over and over again to meet their needs. This reaction sometimes leads to the syndrome of throwing out the baby with the bath water, and develops into "the tyranny of structurelessness", which can be extraordinarily disempowering.

In the vacuum, power struggles, hidden agendas or plain confusion may reign; also the inherent oppressive structures will take over. For instance, in a large rural community — with meetings of 60-100 members — there was great resistance to structured meetings arising from some people's disenchantment with established conservative ways. It led to most of the women and the less articulate or forceful men being unable to be heard at the "tribal" meetings. Things did not change until a core of women insisted on initiating and experimenting with processes that structurally encouraged more equal participation.

In working with activist groups, sometimes I hear the fear expressed that if the focus were taken off the tasks to look into relationships and feelings, a Pandora's box might be opened up. If the group has an attitude that there is no place for reflecting on process and how it is affecting people ("Let's just get on with the job...") things will stay stuck in the old model indefinitely. If it is never legitimate to raise concerns, we lose an opportunity to be truly radical in what we do.

It is good to keep in mind what Hawkhurst and Morrow say in *Living Our Visions — Building Feminist Community*":[5] "Attending to process is not analogous to 'spilling your guts,' it is not carte blanche to dominate the group's time and energy, it is not an assumption that expression of feeling is more important than the business at hand." Rather, attention to process is a recognition that many underlying patterns will take over if ignored. It is a mistake in the longer term to always focus on the urgency of action goals.

INTERGROUP COOPERATION AND ALLIANCE BUILDING

It is as important to build good relationships and cooperation with other groups who have related aims, as it is to build these within your group. Only the current mainstream system benefits from groups remaining isolated and divided. When you are bringing about change which threatens the current structures, divisions and lack of unity will be quickly exploited by critics and those with vested interests in the status quo.

Cooperation can take form anywhere along the continuum, from informal networking by personal contact through to the building of formal coalitions such as these Australian groups: South East Forest Alliance in New South Wales and the Anti US Bases Coalition.

WAYS TO PROMOTE COOPERATION

The simplest ways of enhancing intergroup cooperation are to create contexts for sharing and getting to know each other. It will always work best when bridges are based on personal relationships — the formation of particular allies rather than on a more impersonal, ideological basis. We can take the time to get to know each other as people and appreciate

---

There are many benefits for groups which cooperate in building strong movements for change.

The obvious benefits are:

- By pulling together, you increase your potential influence and enhance each other's strategies or create joint strategies — which better harness people power.
- Scarce resources can be shared and important information pooled.
- Combined fundraising can be more profitable; or, alternatively, finding ways to not compete against each other for fundraising is mutually beneficial.
- Cooperative pressure exerted to stop funding cuts or support funding submissions is more likely to be felt.
- The most important benefit is the morale boost and widening of perspective that comes from perceiving the greater whole and knowing that your group is part of a movement.

The familiar difficulties that arise to prevent cooperation are:

- Underlying feelings of powerlessness get turned into competitive behavior.
- Habits of isolation, or attitudes of always being in opposition, can be turned against anybody whose ideology is not completely aligned.
- Projection of motives and qualities, with subsequent polarization, is unnervingly common among groups who are natural allies. (See Chapter 4.) For instance, two conservation groups were involved in organizing a television film about a conservation issue. Only the much larger and well resourced group was given as a contact at the end of the program. This offended the smaller group, some of whom saw it as some sign of malice on the part of the larger group and proceeded to lobby for sabotage and non-cooperation to an alarming degree. The actual issue which prompted the film became submerged as wounded egos won the day.

---

each other's unique perspective, including reaching out to people who are very different from us in terms of culture, race, religion or class.

It may be useful to have a particular liaison person whose job it is to monitor relationships with other groups, and who looks for opportunities to strengthen ties. It is preferable to choose somebody who doesn't have a lot of inward-focussed responsibilities within the group. Put outreach

> **Other practical ways of building ties are:**
> - Labor swaps, in which you get to work on each other's projects.
> - Newsletter swaps or joint newsletters.
> - Joint training sessions and workshops.
> - Sharing speakers and co-hosting fundraising events.
> - Celebrating victories together or inviting other groups to parties.
>   All these strengthen the sense of the movement that you are part of and help sustain the shared vision.
>   For creating a positive climate, affirmation of one group by another is as important as individual affirmation within groups.
> - Make calls or write letters of congratulations.
> - Put articles in your newsletter about projects that other groups have done.
> - Say what you liked about something the other groups are doing, or express appreciation that they exist.
>   The barriers will tend to crumble quickly when people feel supported and appreciated.

and building alliances on the agenda or have special meetings to focus on this area.

COALITIONS AND ALLIANCES

It is often appropriate to formalize connections with other groups by creating coalitions and alliances.[6] This is not necessarily easy to bring about, as the dilemma is always between the benefits and disadvantages of single- or multi-issue coalitions. Matters become increasingly complicated the broader the groups' bases are.

There is often a tendency to start tearing each other apart over relatively minor points of ideology, and power struggles are all too often the hidden agenda. Power struggles can sometimes be defused by going deeper into understanding the real needs and fears of the parties and then seeing if these can be addressed. (See Mapping Conflict p 66.) Conflict resolution strategies need to be built in as part of the central structure, hopefully without waiting for a major schism to occur before processes are agreed on. It is especially necessary to achieve this in broader based coalitions where total agreement on policy will not be reached.

Although some conflict is inevitable, it is however possible to allow creative ways to maintain a certain degree of diversity — such as by having some non-binding policy statements, stressing areas of agreement and defining spheres of cooperation, shared values and visions. One option is that areas of disagreement be defined and then left alone; another is to bring in a skilled neutral mediator.

Above all, find ways to keep differences in perspective. An awareness of the way projection operates and an understanding of the dynamics of internalized oppression can be very helpful in order to keep things in proportion and depersonalize issues. There is a great deal of learning to be shared about what works and what doesn't work to bring about positive change.

Be selective about whom you invite into a coalition; more isn't always better. Prior research will reveal possible areas of conflict and help form more realistic expectations.

However, some of the strongest and most unexpected gains are made when unlikely alliances between groups are formed, especially groups normally seen to be pitted against one another. A good example of this was in the 1970s in Australia when the NSW Builders Labourers Federation under the leadership of Jack Mundy, instituted "Green Bans". Unions and conservationists aligned together very powerfully to bring about the preservation of old buildings and create green belts around cities. Another example is when real estate agents, dairy farmers and green activists successfully united to oppose the proposed rare earth processing plant in Northern New South Wales.

Nan Nicolson, a horticulturalist and rainforest activist, likens this to the hybrid vigor that develops when two previously unmixed plant or animal species are bred together, producing specimens of outstanding vigor and resistance. Our movements for change could do with all the hybrid vigor they can get!

Animals and Groups

EXERCISES

In this exercise each person in the group can share metaphoric images of how the group is experienced. This makes an interesting start to an evaluation discussion of how the group is going. Each person can answer the following questions:

If you were to describe the group in terms of an animal, or group of animals, what would it/they be?

What would it/they be doing? (For instance: a highly strung dog chasing its tail, or a bunch of hibernating bears waking up in spring and being grumpy with each other, or a plodding work horse that has done the same run for years.)

Checklist — How Well Does Your Group Work Together?

- Is your group's way of operating congruent with its overall vision for the future?
- What is the balance between getting things done and attending to relationships in your group? What would it take to balance this?
- List the areas of skill, talent and knowledge you would ideally like to have in your group, including on your management committee, boards etc. Which of these do you already have? What can you do to recruit new members to fill the gaps?
- Goals and objectives. What do you want to achieve in the next 12 months? Are the goals measurable? How will you know when you have achieved them? Who formed these goals? Have they been reviewed?
- What is the strategy for reaching your goals? Is this linked to an overall campaign? Is this linked with other groups' strategies?
- Is it clear who is responsible for which tasks? What happens if people don't do what they say they will?
- How do you evaluate your programs?
- In what sort of areas does your group lack tools, for instance: decision-making, meeting facilitation, morale boosting, planning,training etc? How might you develop them?
- Is an attitude of experimentation and healthy enquiry encouraged?
- What do you think would add to your enjoyment of belonging to your group?

Affirmations Exercises

These are three ways that groups can affirm and appreciate each other, build self-esteem and group morale. Don't hesitate to give them a try as they work wonderfully in all kinds of groups. However they should not be used to gloss over conflicts that need dealing with.

1. In a circle say something you like or appreciate about the person on your left. Pan around the circle, then go back the other way if you have time.

2. One person at a time: stand in the middle of a circle with your eyes closed, or with your back to the group and "overhear" the rest of the group saying good things about you.

3. Affirmations sheets: Draw your name on a large sheet of paper and

decorate it a little. Now pin or tape the sheet to your back. Move around the room writing appreciations on each other's sheets, which can be signed or not as you wish. Alternately the sheets can be put up around the room for people to write something on them whenever they feel like it.

Checklist on Intergroup Cooperation

- Who are your major allies? How strong are the links between you?
- Who are your necessary or potential allies? What is your plan for enlisting their support?
- Are you aware of your wider circle of supportive people whom you could call on?
- Who is in your network of consultants?
- How is intergroup conflict dealt with?
- How interlinked are your strategies?
- Do you tell people in other groups when you think they are doing a good job?
- Are there physical or human resources which could be shared?
- What is the common ground between your group and your potential allies? What is the larger perspective which unites you?
- Is there any question which you feel you cannot answer? What does this tell you?

Group Feedback Exercise

The purpose of this exercise is to give a simple format to evaluate and share personal experiences of being part of a group. It also helps build understanding and support within a group.[1] Take it in turns, with no interruptions or discussion:

- **What is good about being part of this group for me...**

- **What is hard about being part of this group for me...**

- **What I would like help with is...**

Conflict Resolution Options

The purpose of this exercise is to raise awareness of the many options and strategies there are for resolving conflict, preferably before there is a major conflict in the group. It may stimulate the formation of structures to deal with conflict. Introduce the exercise by pointing out how inevitable it is that groups will experience some conflict at various stages, and the advantage there is in discussing in advance what expectations and options there are for resolving them.

Brainstorm for at least 5 minutes — by writing on a blackboard, whiteboard or sheets of paper in large letters — all the possible options if someone disagrees with someone else or factions are forming; eg. to do "Mapping Conflict" together (see p 66), ask a third person to mediate, put the concerns on the next meeting agenda etc.

Pick a few options and discuss in detail how someone would implement them and when each would be appropriate.

Checking-in

The purpose of "checking-in" is to balance a task-oriented meeting by allowing for the "people" side to be acknowledged. Each person is heard briefly as he or she shares something of a personal nature before the business of the meeting, day or project, gets underway. To share in this way helps us be more present, and gives an opportunity to be inspired by exciting achievements. It allows us to know where each person is coming from by alerting us to the troubles and significant things that have happened in each other's lives, which may affect personal outlooks. Checking-in also tends to build appreciation and support for each other.

I have observed that the process of checking-in can make a very significant difference to the way people relate to each other in groups and the quality of meetings; it is time well spent. The process can also be done at the end or in the middle of events if appropriate — or if there is tension brewing.

Sitting in a circle, allow each person equal time to speak on a topic for instance: "How my day/week/fortnight's... been and how I'm feeling now." It is good to agree on a time period and either have a timekeeper or pass a watch to the person who has just spoken, so s/he can time the next person. Generally each person speaks from 1–3 minutes each, perhaps up to 5 minutes if there is time.

(See also some other creative ways to check-in, p 109)

Speaking in Council

This is a more extended form of "check-in" which allows for deeper sharing and larger themes to emerge. It can be an alternative to a business meeting for a group who meet regularly or as a way of community building at other sorts of gatherings.

The purpose is to share themes, such as how it is to be part of the group, to engage in action, to be facing these times, or whatever else is on our hearts and minds. It is useful also to prepare or debrief after an event such as a nonviolent direct action.

Speaking in council always works best when participants only talk of their own experience and feelings rather than getting abstract or theoretical. It is a ritual which has been used in some form by many tribal cultures such as Australian Aborigines, New Zealand Maoris and Native Americans.

It works well in groups of 7–30 or even much larger groups of over 100 people if there is sufficient self discipline. For groups not used to the process, it works best to have a facilitator. Later as a group gets used to the process and respects the form, members may offer direction more spontaneously. Allow sufficient open ended time in your program planning so the council can come to a natural close rather than running into a time limit.

The group sits in a circle and may use a talking stone (see participation tools, p 100) to ensure each person gets as much time as needed to speak without interruption. After each person in a smaller group has spoken, or after a significant number has spoken in a larger group, it may be apparent that a theme is emerging. A facilitator may sum up the theme and encourage people to expand it further. Sometimes the group just sits in silence until someone else feels moved to speak with no need to direct the process. A sense of sacredness often emerges where the silences are as much part of the sharing as the words. Some groups, influenced by a New Zealand Maori tradition, end each verbal offering with a song or a poem — which they ask the group to join them in if they wish.

Rating Scale — How Well Does Your Group Empower Its Members? see p 164.

NOTES
1. Craig Schindler & Gary Lapid, *The Great Turning — Personal Peace, Global Victory*, Bear & Co Publishing, Santa Fe, New Mexico, 1989.

2. I am indebted to James Bennett-Levy for this analogy.

3. See *Manual For Action*, Martin Jelfs (revised by Sandy Merritt), Action Resources Group, London, 1982.

4. See *Resource Manual For A Living Revolution*, Coover et al, New Society Publishers, Philadelphia, 1978.

5. Hawkhurst & Morrow, *Living Our Visions — Building Feminist Community*.

6. See "Building Coalitions with Other Groups", Cherie Brown in *Tools for Peace*, ed. Neil Wollman, Impact Publishers, San Luis Obispo, California, 1985./(p 157 m/s)

CHAPTER NINE
Facilitating Change

‑‑‑

How often has conflict about leadership and decision-making led to tension in groups you have been part of?

How often is there fear of exercising leadership? Or reaction against it? How often has this led to ineffectiveness?

Leadership and decision-making are thorny issues in many social change groups. In the transition from past patriarchal models there has been much experimentation and as a consequence, many groups have adopted more equitable and participatory methods. In other groups, there have been strong reactions against developing clear structures and processes to replace old paradigms — resulting in inefficiency and very often, conflict.

Old paradigms give us hierarchical models of leadership that are unresponsive to the needs of lower echelons, and resistant to questioning. They also promote their own indispensability, and are typically white, middle class and male. They also give us models of decision-making (if group members are consulted at all) based on pushing through votes, where there are inevitably disgruntled and unsupportive losers.

In the previous chapter we looked at qualities of group culture that empower members and make it more likely that the group will flourish. In this chapter we discuss symptoms and causes of poor leadership; what will bring out the best in leaders; and the advantages of shared leadership for small social change groups. Also we look at the important role of leader as facilitator, and other roles for effective meetings. This leads us into an overview of consensus decision-making.

"Leadership is best when the people say, 'We have done this ourselves'." — *Lao Tzu.*

I would define leadership as a willingness to think about the group as a whole and to offer some direction and influence in helping the group meet its goals. Leadership is necessary in some form, and it inevitably emerges in groups no matter how egalitarian the ideology is, especially whenever there is a perception of a time pressure. If leadership roles are not acknowledged overtly, they inevitably happen covertly or indirectly.

LEADERSHIP

There is no one style of leadership or structure for a group that will suit all situations. Different group structures and styles of leadership will suit different situations.

> *A useful series of questions to ask is:*
> ● Does the leadership style you currently have suit the task functions of your group by efficiently enabling you to achieve your primary goals?
> ● Does it contribute to the maintenance function by promoting a positive and cohesive group feeling?
> ● Does it reflect the kind of society you are wishing to contribute towards?

There are a number of common problems that arise with leadership in social change groups where the leadership is not shared.[1] These problems are symptoms of either poor leadership skills, psychological projection onto leaders from other members (see Chapter 4), internalized oppression (which is a particular form of projection), or structural problems within the group.

Isolation — a dangerous road that often ends up in a blaze of burnout.

The first problem is that of leaders becoming isolated. Some leaders do not consult others because they think they are meant to know already. This also means that they may not admit to vulnerability or ignorance and are therefore less likely to get support or even information. Some won't delegate or share skills, based on an assumption that no one else could do it — leading to the role of overburdened martyr.

Becoming isolated as a leader is a dangerous road that often ends up in a blaze of burnout. The rest of the group is also held back from experiencing their personal power and abilities, and are likely to feel let down by the leader.

Another common problem, particularly among left leaning and New Age groups, is attacks on leaders. Australia has developed a reputation for the "tall poppy syndrome", where many people who start to develop a high profile seem to be subject to intense criticism and discouragement. I'm sure it is true in other countries. Often quite savage criticism emerges from within the group or from related groups, which tends to drive leaders more into rigidity and disillusionment. This criticism may be based on unquestioned and unrealistic expectations of perfection; then when it is realized that the leaders have human needs and/or failings after all, they get attacked quite ferociously.

These attacks may also be based on distress and projection from past experiences with leaders or authorities. Attacks may also derive from unconscious reactions based on past unresolved experiences with leaders and authorities, for instance repeated experiences of punishment at school. (See Chapter 4.)

Another reason for attacks may stem from internalized oppression. This type of attack seems particularly common among women's groups, blacks and minority groups who have experienced a lot of oppression. We may be very critical when the leader is a member of "our group" because we have unknowingly absorbed society's belief that people "like that" should not be leading. Their leadership is contradictory to messages we have received about being unworthy, incapable or that we should remain invisible.

Another problem area in leadership is over-dependency on a particular personality, which leads to discouraging leadership qualities in others. A strong, central, apparently endlessly competent leader can prove disempowering for others. Potential leaders can't see themselves as possessing the needed qualities, nor see how the process works. Over-dependency may be encouraged by leaders who do not wish to have their position threatened.

Potentially every member of a group can lead in some way and can be encouraged to think of her or himself as a leader.

NEEDS OF LEADERS AND POTENTIAL LEADERS

Leaders need a clear mandate to exercise leadership, take initiatives or make decisions. Many groups I have been in tend to be rather unclear about the expectations of people exercising initiative. Leaders may end up being damned if they do take action and damned if they don't. Particularly with community groups it may not always be easy to contact and consult others at all times, and shelving everything until this can be done can be a very inefficient way to operate. Developing clear policy guidelines and discussing expectations before the pressure is on will enable a leader to be more effective.

Leaders need support from members and from other leaders. They need affirmation — to be told what they are doing well. Like all other members they deserve celebration of successes, nurturing and encouragement to look after themselves. Support and accountability groups will provide valuable contexts for these needs to be met. It is a great gift when a leader of a social change group provides a model of someone who can engage wholeheartedly in action, but can also sustain themselves to remain positive and open.

Leaders also need honest feedback so they are kept in touch with the impact of their decisions and actions, and pointers need to be provided for their ongoing growth. Particularly when leadership is shared, feedback needs to be given concerning areas to strengthen, or qualities to tone down. This will always be more effective as constructive criticism rather than attack. It is also more helpful when it is specific to a particular situation or behavior.

A group is in danger when members feel they cannot be honest with leaders for fear of hurting egos, fear of retaliation or lack of acceptance.

SHARED LEADERSHIP

Leadership need not be confined to one particular person, as feminist groups particularly have found.[2] It can be a role/function that rotates within the group: for instance, as meeting facilitator, PR spokesperson, team coordinator. Another model is that aspects of the roles of leadership are clearly delineated and then distributed among a number of people. This does not assume everyone has the same skills, but it is an attempt to find a balance between recognizing already developed skills and talents in some, and fostering undeveloped abilities in others. This becomes a longer term investment in healthy social change organizations with an empowered membership, rather than settling for an arrangement suiting short-term expediency (or following old habits and assumptions).

A lot of leadership is not, in fact, in the overt form of, "now focus on me — I'm the leader" style. Subtler influencers who foster group cohesion, build morale and take responsibility for unspectacular but essential things, often go unrecognized as exercising leadership of a kind and are undervalued. These roles traditionally fall to women in mixed groups, while the more prominent directive tasks traditionally have gone to men and been more highly valued. In our groups we should be seeking to develop skills in both the task and relationship areas, in both men and women.

However, putting too strong an emphasis on the idea that everyone *is* equal or on the demand that everyone *should* be equal can be experienced by some members as a burden, and is in practice unrealistic. It leads to resentment when people do not live up to the expectation. It can also be that people do not take responsibility for finding what is right for themselves, developing their own abilities or accepting themselves and others. I have noticed that expecting equality sometimes backfires, with people resenting or feeling threatened by anyone taking initiative or developing excellence in some area.

Finding and experimenting with new forms of leadership and ways of working together, is central to our effectiveness in bringing about lasting positive social change.

FACILITATING MEETINGS

Meetings often succeed or fail according to the skills of the leader or facilitator. You can judge the success of meetings on the two important dimensions — task and maintenance.

> Task — What got done? Did you get the needed results? Did
> problems get solved and things planned to meet objectives?
> Maintenance — How did it get done? How did people feel and how
> will this affect morale and group cohesion? Did the meeting
> make good use of the pooled talents? Was it enjoyable?

One of the most vital roles for at least one person to play at a meeting is that of the facilitator. Lack of facilitation, or poorly facilitated meetings, add more to the frustration levels within a group than anything else. This is a role that can be learnt. It can also be rotated amongst group members so more people develop the skills and the group is not reliant on a few individuals to function effectively. It is well worth conducting training, aside from normal meeting times, to practice facilitation skills.

There are other leadership roles which can be rotated. (See Table 3)

It can be useful to have co-facilitators, who can take over if the facilitator needs to step out of her/his role because of a wish to participate in the discussion, or to have a break, or because more back-up is needed when there is a build-up of tension, conflict or confusion.

THE QUALITIES OF GOOD FACILITATORS: (Table 1)

Neutrality. Though they may contribute to the discussion and make suggestions, they should not manipulate the meeting to bring about a particular outcome.

Good listening skills including reflective listening and strategic questioning.

Respect for the participants and confidence that consensus can be reached and good solutions found.

Interest in what people have to offer.

Assertiveness that is not overbearing — to know when to intervene decisively and give some direction to the meeting.

Clear thinking and observation of the whole group. This requires a split attention to the content of the discussion and the process (ie. how this is affecting group members).

An understanding of the overall objectives of the group.

CONSENSUS DECISION-MAKING

Of all the decisionmaking processes consensus is most consistent with this model of shared leadership. Using this process means that each person potentially has to think about the group's needs and take responsibility for guiding and following through decisions.

> **THE ROLE OF A MEETING FACILITATOR:** (Table 2)
>
> 1. See that an agenda is formed and agreed on, preferably with time allocations for each item, and set a realistic finishing time. If the full consensus process is going to be used, there needs to be allowance for extra time to go deeper into the issue if necessary.
> 2. Ensure that the other roles such as recorders, timekeepers etc. are covered.
> 3. Regulate the flow of discussion so it is open and balanced and there is equal opportunity for participation by all. It is helpful to encourage some pauses for issues to be thought about or to allow less articulate people to speak up.
> 4. Keep the group focussed on one item at a time until decisions are reached — even if the decision is to shelve it for some other time. Decisions on action steps should include what, how, who, when and where.
> 5. Make sure the participants are using the most effective means of accomplishing tasks and reaching decisions, eg. brainstorming options, forming small groups for discussion, delegating to committees, suggesting a "go around" etc.
> 6. Sum up and provide some satisfying closure to the meeting.

Consensus tends to engender greater commitment.

Consensus is the process I have had the most experience with in community groups and believe has the greatest potential — even though it seems to be one of the least understood and most sloppily applied procedures. However, when it is properly applied it is not only a good decision-making technique but it also fosters unity and understanding. Consensus tends to engender greater commitment to the decisions taken than a voting process where there are losers.

Consensus is a very old process; it has been used by indigenous tribes and cultures for thousands of years. In our culture, the Society of Friends (Quakers) has used it for over 300 years. It has been successfully applied even to very large gatherings of hundreds of people such as the Women's Action at the Pine Gap United States Base in Central Australia in 1984. At this gathering, time was taken to discuss strategies and reach consensus decisions about actions by a combination of small groups feeding back to the whole group and large gatherings of the whole camp.

"Consensus is based on the belief that each person has some part of the truth and no one has all of it, no matter how much we would like to believe so, and on a respect for all persons involved in the decision that is being considered . . . the process is a search for the very best solutions to whatever is the problem."[3]

OTHER LEADERSHIP ROLES IN MEETINGS (Table 3)

These can also be rotated between group members.

Vibeswatcher

Their job is to watch the energy level of the participants and offer some intervention if it gets too low, or too high such as by suggesting a break, a stretch or a game.

Notetaker/Recorder

This role is important in order to keep track of decisions, take minutes, collect reports, and also to draw attention to incomplete decisions; for instance: who was going to contact so and so?

Timekeeper

This role draws attention to an agreed time frame and keeps the group to it, negotiating extensions if needed.

Convener/Coordinator

Having this as a separate role assists the facilitators to remain centered in themselves. Conveners can take care of the venue, see there are enough chairs, equipment, refreshments and notices and gather people to start on time.

Listening Committee

In large gatherings that go over an extended period of time, this small group makes itself available, especially in the breaks, to hear complaints, take suggestions and feedback. The committee either sort out the situation as best they can or feed the information back to the organizers and facilitators. It is a constructive way to deal with undercurrents of dissatisfaction and makes it easier for participants to raise concerns rather than having to speak out in the large group.

Consensus requires a group that is willing to work together and trust there is a solution, as well as patience and perseverance. It requires us to come to meetings with our minds not fixed on a particular solution or position; in the light of hearing all the possible positions we may modify ours. Everyone present must get (or potentially have) the opportunity to present ideas and solutions, while being listened to with respect.

Generally the process flows smoothly and relatively quickly, particularly when underlying feelings and personality issues are being dealt with by other processes. With many of the potential snags removed, the way is cleared for a more rational consideration of the actual issues for decision. However sometimes a slower and more sensitive process is required, especially while a group is developing the skills required for consensus decision-making.

Factors which make the process more difficult for an inexperienced group are: first, urgency to make important decisions or shortage of time due to an overfull meeting agenda; secondly, changing membership attending meetings — this slows the development of the process, the building of trust and the acquisition of skills. However, by allowing enough time, avoiding the urgency trap and orienting people fully, these difficulties will be eased.

THE CONSENSUS PROCESS

The process begins with a statement of the issue or problem given clearly and in an unbiased way, eg. "The issue is: shall we blockade the mine site?" or "The issue is: how shall we blockade the mine site?"

The facilitator then invites and regulates discussion, and clarifies proposals put forward, not letting anyone dominate and encouraging reticent members to speak. It can be very fruitful to pause for reflective silence, particularly on difficult decisions. People who do not agree with a proposal are invited to speak as well as those who do. The facilitator needs to state and restate the position of the meeting as it appears to be emerging until agreement is reached. Everyone need not think uniformly on the issue. What generally eventuates is that everyone agrees to go along with the decision. It implies a contract to abide by the decision and not undermine it. Sometimes the meeting gets to the point where everyone agrees except one or two people. There are three options at this juncture:

a) See whether the individuals are willing to "step aside". This means they do not agree with the decision but they do not feel it is fundamentally wrong, and will accept it proceeding. (They may be satisfied by having their reticence recorded in the notes.)

Some people remain silent because they don't want to rock the boat.

b) The issue gets laid aside for another time. Having more time to reflect, new perspectives may come to light. The need for the decision is not always more important than unity. Often we allow ourselves to be time pressured into accepting inferior solutions and overriding dissatisfactions, which later fester.

c) Individuals can choose to stop the meeting from moving forward or "block consensus". In my experience it happens rarely, though it is often feared by those not used to using consensus. At this point sensitive exploration of the reasons for individuals assuming this position is required and the group needs to take an open look at the merit of their position. People would block consensus when they believe "that the decision is basically wrong and they cannot in conscience let it go forward". Often it turns out they are speaking for others who have remained silent because they don't want to rock the boat. An important element, therefore, is being represented.

If, however, particular members find themselves at odds with the group consistently, maybe they need to consider whether they are in the wrong group.

Some groups have a "back-up" system of reverting to a vote (usually requiring at least ¾ or ⅔ majority) if consensus is not reached after a period of time. Though this may seem pragmatic, it can have the effect of lessening the motivation to keep grappling with consensus forming and the considerable long-term benefits of doing so. The group needs to be very clear about how and under what circumstances it would revert to a vote.

It is very worthwhile to evaluate meetings regularly as a matter of course. **EVALUATION** It is preferable to do so for about 5 minutes at the end of each meeting. The way of meeting is thus constantly being refined, rather than waiting till everyone is so dissatisfied that the group goes into decline. This process also allows people in the various leadership roles to receive feedback that will enhance their skills. It is 5 minutes well spent. (*see* Evaluation Exercises p 101.)

To be effective change agents in groups that empower our members, we need to question and continually refine the way in which leadership is exercised and decisions reached. This applies to the day-to-day running of groups and especially meetings. Such commitment to the microcosm of the group is a major contribution to building a world that is consistent with our dreams.

EXERCISES

Leadership Checklist

- What style of leadership does your group have? What are the advantages and disadvantages of this for your organization?
- Who in particular has power and influence in your group? Is this official or unofficial?
- What would happen if key people were to leave your group?
- What roles could you rotate and what else could your group do to spread leadership?
- What are you doing to encourage leadership skills in your members?
- How do you support people who exercise leadership in your group?

Discussion Regulators

FISHBOWL

The purpose of this exercise is to make a discussion in a large group (8–50) proceed more smoothly and increase the likelihood that people listen to one another. It also makes it very obvious if somebody is taking more than his or her share of the talking time.

The group sits in a circle with 4–7 chairs or cushions in an inner circle. One chair in the inner circle (and only one) remains empty at all times, while the others are taken by rotating group members who wish to speak.

The discussion is started by those who are ready to join the inner circle. Allow 5 minutes or so for the discussion to get going; then anyone from the outer circle can come into the empty chair, but this means one person from the inner circle must leave and rejoin the outer circle, creating another empty chair. Only those in the center can speak.

TALKING STONE

The purpose of this tool is to ensure that in a discussion only one person speaks at a time and that the speakers are ensured they cannot be interrupted, even if they need a moment's silence or if they speak slowly. This also helps the quality of listening and decreases polarization. It works in groups from 3–50.

With the group sitting in a circle, an object (such as a smooth stone, a crystal or even a coke bottle) is passed either randomly round the circle (to whoever indicates a readiness to speak), or in turns around the circle. Only the person with the talking stone can speak. Another version of this is that the stone is placed and replaced into the center of the circle rather than handed to the next person.

MATCHSTICKS

The purpose of this discussion regulator is to even out the participation rates in a discussion and make people consider carefully what they contribute, as they initially only get limited opportunities to speak. It works in groups from 3–50.

Hand out 2–6 matchsticks (or other tokens) to each person, the number being dependent on the size of the group and the time available. Each time someone speaks they put their token aside or in the middle. When a participant runs out of tokens they cannot speak. When all who wish to have used up their tokens, the discussion can then proceed more loosely.

Evaluation tools are very useful after meetings, workshops, trainings or actions to enable us to refine what we do and find out if our objectives were reached. It also provides an opportunity to affirm what went well, which adds to the positive feelings and motivation. Evaluating allows expressions of dissatisfaction at the time, rather than finding out about them indirectly later — or not at all. It generates specific information for future use, so it is helpful to keep notes to refer to later. There are numerous ways of conducting evaluations. The few that are offered here can be adapted to the needs of the situation.

Evaluation Exercises

It seems to work best if someone other than the person who led the event does the evaluation, because it is then easier for participants to express dissatisfaction.

BRAINSTORM EVALUATIONS

A) Divide a wall chart or large sheet of paper into three columns and brainstorm:

> **Things that went well/ were useful**
> **Things that didn't work well/ were not useful**
> **Suggestions for next time/improvements**

B) Another variation is to brainstorm comments on:

> **What was covered (content)**
> **How well the material was covered (process)**

EVALUATION SHEETS

Either hand out prepared evaluation sheets or read out questions to the group to answer on a sheet of paper. These are then collected for later analysis. Example questions are:

What were the most valuable things for you about this event/ training/meeting...?

Rating Scale — Leadership and Decision Making

1. LEADERSHIP ROLES: How clear are leadership roles in your group (even if shared/rotated?)

Absence of clear
leadership, laissez faire
Clear
leadership roles

2. DEVELOPING NEW LEADERSHIP: Is attention given to encouraging leadership skills among members?

No encouragement
High degree of
encouragement

3. CRITICISM: Are leaders attacked or criticized (rather than given constructive feedback)?

High degree of destructive criticism
High degree of
constructive feedback

4. SUPPORT: Are those exercising leadership given support and encouragement?

Unsupported, isolated
and/or discouraged
Highly supported,
valued, and encouraged

5. FEEDBACK & EVALUATION: Is there evaluative feedback given to those in leadership?

No feedback given,
not accountable
High degree of
accountability

6. MEETINGS: What is the overall quality of your meetings?

Poor — ineffective, hard
Excellent — effective
& enjoyable

7. DECISION MAKING: Overall how satisfied are you with the group's processes for decision making?

Not at all satisfied
Highly satisfied

What was the least valuable?
Did you find it easy to participate in this meeting?
What suggestions do you have for improving . . . ?
These sheets can either be signed or anonymous.

RATING SCALES

You may wish to design a rating scale to evaluate the questions of interest to you. Among points to bear in mind are: make sure that the questions are unambiguous; that they cover the whole domain of the subject of interest; that they are worded appropriately for the rating scale being used (eg.it is no good asking a yes/no question if you are using a 5 point rating scale). Make sure that the points on the rating scale are approximately equidistant, eg. a 5 point scale of Very Bad, Bad, Average, Good, Very Good is equidistant, a 3 point scale — Very Bad, Good, Very Good is not. If you wish to compute a total score, make sure the questions are asked so that answers of the same type (eg. positive) receive a similar (high) score. Most importantly, do a dummy run with the rating scale to iron out deficiencies before putting it to use.

OBJECTIVE BASED EVALUATIONS

At the beginning of a project, a workshop or period of time, clear objectives can be set which give a basis to evaluate performance, eg. "To conduct a survey of all households in The Channon on attitudes towards the proposed Tavern — by August" or "That participants will set-self care goals for the next two months". If this is to be of value it is essential that the objective is worded in such a way that it is clear when it has been achieved.

NOTES
1. Harvey Jackins, *The Enjoyment Of Leadership*, Rational Island Publishers, Seattle, 1987.

2. See *Leadership For Change — Towards A Feminist Model* by Bruce Kokopeli & George Lakey, New Society Publishers, Philadelphia.

3. Caroline Estes, "Consensus" in *In Context*, Autumn, 1984.

Support and Accountability Groups

Has your concern about a social issue ever made you feel lonely or isolated?

Do you have trouble getting going? Do you lack confidence?

Do you find it hard to think clearly about your social change commitment and sort through priorities?

Are there some issues in your local action group that tempt you to give up and drop out?

Do the questions above relate to familiar difficulties?

It is not easy going against the mainstream. Forming a support and accountability group is a good tool for resolving these difficulties. As Jan McNicol, a nonviolent action trainer from Brisbane, says: "Without a support network, I find I get further away from social change things and more into conventional society. Without the direct personal support for the things I am about, it is hard for me to maintain my truth."

The purpose of a support and accountability group is to focus on you as an individual and your social change work rather than to discuss joint action projects. With the support and attention of 2–6 others, this focus provides a unique opportunity to dissolve barriers to effective action and encourages you to expand into your potential. It can also help you choose your direction and plan strategies. Such a group takes a holistic approach which allows reflection on all the dimensions of our lives — emotional, political, spiritual and material.

The members, in turn, choose what is most important for them to focus on and state what they want from the rest of the group. For instance, at our group Bobbi Allen was tired after running some intensive trainings, so asked for massage; Kath Fisher wanted some suggestions on a workshop she was planning to run; and I wanted to set some goals and priorities for the coming months.

Accountability develops as members remind each other of former resolutions or insights, checking back on commitments made and giving solid back-up to keep attention on blind spots.

At first I groaned at the idea of another meeting to attend, but I have found the extra hours are repaid in terms of increased effectiveness in my work and an added sense of well-being and connectedness with others. Some other groups I belonged to did offer some support but they were large, with different people attending each time. Sometimes a few people did most of the talking. Other groups were solely task-oriented. The busy rush of daily life with family and friends does not often offer the opportunity for thoughtful reflection on a long-term personal strategy for my social change work.

The easiest way to start is to decide to have one, then personally invite the people you would like to be in your group. Pick people you are most likely to feel comfortable with and can trust to listen and support you, as well as those who share your political perspective. Explain clearly what it is you are after. Choose people with whom you have a sense of relative equality or "peerness". Groups with very unequal skills or experience may not work well. You are likely to regret asking people you feel you "ought" but with whom you don't actually feel comfortable.

Keep going until you have 3–4 who seem to have the same basic goals, expectations or needs for the group. Four or five is a good number — a larger group means less focus time, though it may be possible to break a larger group of 7–10 into smaller ones for "focus time".

Initial meetings should give some attention to making clear agreements and structures, getting-to-know-each-other time and building trust. If you do not already know each other well, sharing stories can be an interesting way to start — stories of your awareness of the issue you are working on or the history of your political activism. (See Useful Exercises for New Support Groups p 110.) It will enhance the effectiveness of the group if you can get a commitment to come for a fixed number of meetings and notify someone if you cannot attend a particular meeting. This simple agreement helps prevent energy and morale evaporating.

Affirm that this type of group is primarily support for action — though paradoxically this may mean supporting activists to stop acting for awhile! If there is a continual drift into personal issue therapy, (though obviously this is very useful, it may not be the right setting), general chatting, or a lot of intellectualizing, the potential of the group as a social change tool will be watered down.

HOW TO SET UP A SUPPORT AND ACCOUNT- ABILITY GROUP

STRUCTURE

Having a structure which is agreed upon and moved through crisply, is much more effective than a "see what comes up" approach.

A structure which we are using for our support/accountability group is, we:

- Meet fortnightly for 2½ to 3 hours.
- Gather together for 15 minutes before starting to have a cup of tea and chat.
- Focus activity for 5 minutes or so: for example, meditation, reading an inspiring quote or a song.
- Start with a check-in: a round of sharing how work, or life generally, has been since last time and how we are feeling right now; or we share something new and good. (Keep it crisp — maximum of 3–5 minutes each.)
- Divide up the focus time. This could be 30 minutes each for 4 people, or 'short 'n' longs': 2 people have 40 minutes each, then 2 people have 20 minutes each with a change over next meeting.
- Breaks for a stretch or a quick game are added as needed.
- Evaluate the meeting: Was it satisfactory? Are there possible changes to agreements or structure? Make the next meeting arrangements and announcements.
- Choose some suitable close : A song, sharing foot-rubs, a good joke . . . Use your imagination.

Variations. This format can be jazzed up if you have time; for instance: a relaxation exercise, a creative visualization, any of the exercises from this book or a shared meal. Other possibilities are: set aside time for general discussion on a chosen topic or have some study group time. It could become a picnic or a whole day's program occasionally.

MAKING THE GROUP WORK

Clear agreements. At the beginning, decide exactly what you want to do together, how often, how long, how to deal with lateness.

Confidentiality is very necessary for building trust. Make a clear commitment that sensitive personal matters raised in the group will not get discussed outside the group.

Start and finish on time. This will make it more likely that members keep attending. Waffly meetings that start and finish late are the bane of a busy person's life!

Equal time for each person to speak and have the focus of attention, is a worthwhile principle to stick to, although it may feel a little contrived at times.

Clarity of purpose. Resist the temptation to get sidetracked. Stay with the person whose turn it is and on his/her stated topic.

Practice good listening. This is a key element. (See Chapter 5.) You don't need to be an expert counselor to be very effective as a support person. Good listening allows the focus person to think out loud, explore feelings and clarify dilemmas. It enables participants to listen more carefully to themselves. It is surprising how often this is enough.

Encouragement and affirmation. Sometimes this is discouragingly absent from daily life; many of us have a corrosive tendency to criticize ourselves and each other, or to think that our efforts are futile. I believe the lack of self- and mutual affirmation and recognition of success is a major factor in burnout. To hear someone say "You can do it!" or "That worked well" or even "You are doing ENOUGH!" is a pleasant antidote to the self-doubting voices inside our own heads.

Ask *pertinent, strategic questions* to encourage clarity on each person's objectives and how to reach them. This may have a personal focus such as "What's your next step?" "What's holding you back?" "What is the most important thing for you?" etc. Or the questions may have primarily a political focus to clarify suitable tactics and action planning, such as "What stage is the campaign up to?", "Are there historical precedents to consider?", or "Who are the major allies?".

Encouraging skills and study. These sorts of groups help identify skills needed and areas for development. For instance these might be: assertiveness training (which can be practiced by role playing in the group) or public speaking (a suitable course could be suggested). Other needs can be identified for study and research into such things as a strategic overview of the stages of social movements,[2] nonviolent tactics or an historical perspective on the issue you are working with, etc. Perhaps some separate study group time would be appropriate.

Encouraging self-care is an important role the group can have. Urge people to rest and renew sufficiently between activities.

Giving support may not always mean just being "nice".

Silence. Encourage the focus person to pause occasionally, to go within, to reflect without interruption. Pausing before you speak as a non-focus participant can make it easier for a quieter and non-assertive person to participate.

Providing challenge and feedback. Giving support may not always mean just being "nice". A gentle and skilful challenge or honest feedback may be fruitful. "Are you really the only one who can do that?" "I notice that's very like the way you relate to your father — would you like to explore this further?" The trust level needs to be fairly high, and the challenging should be done judiciously and sensitively. It doesn't need to turn into an encounter group. The support group is an opportunity to practice receiving feedback — not to deflect the positive or get defensive about the negative. Challenge could also mean encouraging others to be bolder in their action.

It nearly always helps when you can encourage someone to get specific, speak directly and personally, keep it concrete, and encourage practical outcomes.

Therapeutic techniques.[3] Sometimes the drawing out and exploration of deeper feelings can be useful if you have the time and the skills. My group encouraged me to dialogue with my old typing teacher — telling her to "get off my back", among other things, in order to work on an apparent block about becoming more competent on the word processor.

Providing an opportunity in the group to do some "despair work" (See Chapter 1) could liberate a lot of energy tied up in grief or anger about the state of the planet.[4] The group need not be working at this deeper level to still be very effective. There may be varying levels of skill in using these techniques in the group.

Deal with conflicts as they arise. Letting resentments build will inevitably undermine the group. These sorts of groups are ideal training grounds for conflict resolution — which is an essential social action tool.

No recruiting for your cause from this support group unless people offer.

We often end our focus time by making a homework commitment — something to do before next time that will further our goals or put a new decision into practice. Commitments I have made are: "I will list in detail the steps involved in the project"; "I will take time out for myself, like a trip to the beach next Saturday"; "I will write three letters to politicians regarding recent cuts to women's services in the next week".It is good to review these at the next meeting. Periodically it is valuable to focus on long term strategies, goals and directions.

As children, many of us did not have role models of how to give and receive good support, so it is something we need to learn and practice.

"My support group keeps me from getting one-eyed."

Being involved in social change work can sometimes feel like a fish swimming upstream. Much of it is unpaid, unpopular and perceived as "unpatriotic"! Burnout of activists is rife and a sense of isolation can be acute. If our commitment to social change is for a lifetime, then it will involve much soul searching, drawing on deeper energies and motivations, and the gradual development of congruency between our beliefs and actions and all aspects of our lives — our relationships, our means of livelihood, our pattern of consumption and our priorities. Being involved in a support group can be an opportunity for more integration of the personal and political, balancing the needs of the whole of your being and reflecting consciously on the layers of your life.

Pat Fleming, a British environmentalist working on computer information networking, said: "For me my support group is a welcome oasis of friends whose opinions I value. I can certainly take my concerns about my work and other circumstances in my life for support and reflection. I review my work and find ways to keep it fresh. It keeps me from getting one-eyed. There is a lightness and depth in what we do."

EXERCISES

Creative Check-ins:

I learnt these check-in exercises at the Drama Action Centre in Sydney from Bridgit Brandon and Peter Hall.

Their purpose is to "check-in" with your group in light, fun ways, and to warm up to being together.

LAST WEEK AS A PANTOMIME

- Using sounds, gibberish words, movement and dance, take it in turns to give a short presentation that captures the quality of your previous week. Exaggerate your movements and gestures. Don't be shy. Was it frantic, boring, exciting, confusing?

IF I WERE A MEAL

- If you were a meal, what might you be right now? (eg. a plate of cold spaghetti or dish of slightly over-ripe avocados with lumpy bits...)

LANDSCAPES

- If you were a landscape what would you be right now? (eg. a freeway under construction or a manicured English rose garden...)

BOOK OR FILM TITLES

- If you had a book or film title that described how your life had been since last meeting, what would it be? (eg. "Life on a Roller Coaster!" "The Soap Opera on High Street" or "Hum Drum and Some Pleasant Surprises".)

Useful Exercises for New Support Groups

Checking-in (See p 89 & 109)
Last week as a pantomime (See p 109)
Telling short histories of your involvement in social issues.
Listening skills exercises (See p 51)
Telling our waking up stories (See p 7)
Making a Difference (See p 19)
Empowerment Stories (See p 23)
Open sentences on Our Concerns (See p 76)
Web chart for identifying stressors (See p 132)
Your Support — Community Collage (See p 33)
Setting and Evaluating Goals Worksheet (See p 111)

Strengthening Your Determination*

The purpose of this exercise is to strengthen your determination to complete an important task, and to develop assertiveness to deal with things that might pull you off course. The tone need not get too serious! It can be done in pairs or small groups.

In a small group, appoint one person to read the instructions and direct the process. The exercise has 4 sections. Take it in turns to be the focus person and complete these steps:

1. Begin by relaxing, closing your eyes and visualizing a goal that you really want to achieve ... (Pause) ... Now imagine how you will feel when you have achieved that goal. Let yourself feel the sense of satisfaction, excitement and achievement right though your body ... (Pause) ...

2. Now tell your partner/s about your intended goal and also the sorts of things you might allow to pull you off course. Coach your partners a little about personifying the pressures in your life. (3–5 minutes)

3. Now identify a spot at the other end of the room that would signify reaching your goal. Stand up, prepare yourself with determination to get there. Start slowly and deliberately moving towards your goal, while your partner/s try to push you aside or restrain you. (This should be done gently, without making it impossible for the focus person to move.) Partners may also find words that could interrupt

SETTING AND EVALUATING GOALS WORKSHEET

The purpose of this worksheet is to give a framework for a thorough evaluation of your work. Consider photocopying this page, keeping one empty one as a master sheet. It will be most helpful if it is used regularly. It can be used alone or as a basis for discussion with others.

1. *Which of your goals did you reach in the last month?*

2. *What else has been achieved that you can give yourself credit for?*

3. *What has your quality or attitude of mind been towards yourself and others? Did you enjoy what you did? Did you take care of yourself?*

4. a) *What areas need more attention, either because they are unfinished, unresolved or unsatisfactory?*
   b) *What do you need to do about these omissions?*
   c) *Who or what might be of assistance?*

5. *What are your goals for the next month (including some fun things)?*

What?	Who else is involved?	When By?

this progress, such as: "What about me? I'm your other job" or " But have you really got all the skills?", "The kids need more time", "Do you really want this?" or whatever is appropriate. Use your intuition to make it fuller and to find the appropriate soft spots.

You, as the person "running the gauntlet", are encouraged to answer back and to push through regardless. It is particularly effective when you find your strength in the pelvis and legs, to assist determinedly pushing through. (Approximately 5 minutes)

4. When you reach your goal point, discuss what it felt like and what you discovered by doing the exercise. Specifically identify the things that made you feel like giving up. What do you need to do to surmount these inner and outer obstacles? What sort of support and accountability will help you maintain your direction? (5 minutes). Finish by thanking your partners. Then swap roles.

* Be aware that some people may not feel comfortable with the physical contact and restraint involved in this exercise. It should always be optional.

Clarifying Your Social Change Path

The purpose of this series of questions is to clarify what direction you have the most enthusiasm and inspiration for. It is important to find a balance in this long-term planning between bold, courageous thinking and what is possible.

The questions can be worked through on your own or in pairs. An encouraging and discriminating listener can be of assistance to bring out your best. If you are doing this exercise with a partner, take turns to ask this series of questions and take notes of your partner's responses. When the series is complete, read back the responses to the speaker (who may want to keep the sheet for later reference). The partners then swap roles. Allow at least 30–40 minutes per person to answer questions, (3–5 minutes per question). With additional group discussion time at the end, the exercise takes approximately 1½ hours.

1. **What is the issue (or issues) closest to your heart? Where do your real passions and interests lie?**
2. **What would you love to do/see happen about this?**
3. **Considering your talents and previous experiences, what is your unique and specific contribution? What could be your job?**
4. **If you had the courage where would you really like this to lead in future, say 12 months from now? 5 years from now?**
5. **Who would you love to join forces with?**

6. What learning, information, resources or support do you need in order to make this a reality?

7. How might you sabotage yourself from succeeding? What are your best strategies for not doing this?

8. If you were helping a much loved friend make these decisions, what practical and encouraging advice would you give? (On the basis of this advice, is there anything about your previous responses you may need to modify?)

9. What are your first steps?

(If there is time remaining, continue becoming more specific about planning and setting goals within a time-frame.)

Consultancy or "Clearness" Meetings

This is a very fruitful process[5] that gives a structure to asking for support and feedback from people who you trust will think about your best interests. It is valuable if you are not part of an ongoing support group or if you need more time than your group usually allows. It can assist you to make an important decision, clarify a direction or think through a project. It involves inviting 2–5 people, friends or colleagues who know you well and care about you — people who you can rely on to listen well, support you and think clearly and objectively about the issues.

Preparation.
- Invite your team of consultants.
- Clarify your needs and priorities, by writing and talking to people. Think about an agenda.
- Collect any relevant information.
- Deal with any upset or stress associated with the decisions.

At the meeting.
- Select a facilitator who will keep an overview of the process, ensure the focus stays with you, and make sure you are getting what you need.
- Select a notetaker to record main points, draw up charts with pros and cons etc.
- Form an agenda and make time allocations.
- Make it clear to your team when you want to talk and when you want feedback or advice.

Sample agenda.
- Opening activity (eg.shoulder rubs, song) 5 minutes.
- Check-in for each person. (see p 89)
- Succinctly outline your needs and purpose for the meeting
- Outline what you would like from your team.
- Outline the issue/s, including any relevant background information.
- Answer any questions of clarification.

- Form an agenda of issues, then proceed through it with some breaks as needed, (drink, stretch, a game etc.).
- Set goals, plan next steps and any follow-up needed.
- Share some appreciations and affirmations of each other.
- Evaluate the meeting — 5 minutes.
- Do a closing activity.

NOTES

1. Tova Green et al. *Keeping Us Going — A Manual On Support Groups for Activists*. Published by Interhelp USA, 1986. Some of the content of this chapter was drawn from this helpful publication.

2. See *The Practical Strategist* by Bill Moyer, July 1990 or *The Map Training Manual*, October 1990. Published by Social Movement Empowerment Project (see resource section).

3. A good introduction to and overview of therapeutic techniques to use in groups such as this can be found in *In Our Own Hands — A Book of Self Help Therapy* by Sheila Ernst & Lucy Goodison. The Women's Press, London, 1981.

4. See *Despair And Personal Power In The Nuclear Age* by Joanna Macy, New Society Publishers Philadelphia, USA, 1983 and *Thinking Like A Mountain* by John Seed, Joanna Macy, Pat Fleming & Arne Naess. New Society Publishers, 1988.

5. For a fuller explanation of this process and variations, see the booklet by Peter Woodrow, *Clearness: Processes For Supporting Individuals And Groups In Decision Making*, New Society Publishers, Philadelphia.

Other Ways of Getting Support

If setting up a support and accountability group doesn't seem feasible, consider these other options:

- Weekly **phone check-in** with an ally (someone who understands and supports your work).
- Post your **evaluation sheet** to a colleague regularly and have them post their sheet to you.
- Invite a selection of friends and colleagues to a **consultancy** or **"clearness" problem-solving session**. Or do a longer range evaluation and make plans. (See Consultancy or Clearness meetings p 113)
- Structure in **support group time at conferences, workshops and meetings**, where the emphasis is on personal sharing. Remember the equal time principle.
- Recognize that all people in groups need personal nourishment and build that into business meetings with **"Check-ins"** which are personal report times. Also share victory moments, celebrations and compliments as part of the agenda.
- Periodically instead of a business meeting you could **"Speak in Council"** with your group. (See p 89)
- **Form caucuses and interest groups** at conferences, gatherings or in your workplace. In these groups you can focus on areas of common interest and concern, as well as cross-pollinating ideas and information.
- Don't wait for someone else to do it: **organize seminars and workshops** around themes that interest or inspire you. Invite facilitators to run them if you do not feel confident.
- Organize a **meal, retreat or weekend away** with people with whom you don't spend enough time normally, but who share your interests.
- Organize a **Networking Party**: (I learnt these exercises at an Interhelp gathering facilitated by Fran Peavey.) Invite a group of people who have similar interests for an evening. All get to introduce themselves and what they do, then say what they need and what they could offer others. Another variation on this is to write down what are your interests, needs and offerings on a sheet of paper. Pin the sheet to your chest then move around among the group — greeting, reading each other's sheets and discussing mutual interests. This may lead to forming ways to cooperate.

Preventing Burnout

CHAPTER ELEVEN
Survival Tactics
(HOW TO SPARK WITHOUT INCINERATION)

Twice in my life I have experienced periods of mounting urgency and obsession with social action projects. This was coupled with a profound lethargy and deep exhaustion that a few days off did not relieve. I was not able to keep much perspective on my life. I did know, however, it was getting out of balance. Work took up nearly all of my time, one way or another. I kept saying "I can't stop now 'cos I gotta..."

I was getting sick more often and feeling more resentful particularly towards anybody who wanted something from me. Generally the feeling was of being shrivelled up inside, but pushing on regardless.

I did not realize then that I was suffering from burnout, a prolonged stress reaction. It probably would have helped had I realized that these types of symptoms are common among those who work in human services, such as health and welfare workers, police, teachers, ministry and people active in other forms of social change movements, but it can occur in any activity.

This section will focus on the conditions and dynamics that affect people active in social change movements, such as peace workers, environmentalists, social justice and community development workers. These pressures are common whether the activists are voluntary, semi-voluntary or employed by a community based group.

Sometimes the expression "burnout" is used quite superficially. For example it can be used to mean "I'm tired", as in "I'm feeling a bit burnt-out today". Sometimes cures are suggested glibly, as if it were just a simple and obvious matter. This usage of the expression "burnout" denies the depth of the anguish — the emotional and physical toll on the person experiencing full blown burnout.

Some people may experience burnout as a temporary malaise, make appropriate adjustments and continue on. For others burning-out means a stress related disease producing a major life crisis from which they may never fully recover. If the issues remain unresolved, the stressed person

"Burnout is a psychological metaphor — what has been damaged in the flames is the soul. Our souls and our bodies interact so closely that when one is damaged the other is usually in trouble too." — Patricia Vigderman.

may avoid the field of social action altogether, retreating into intractable cynicism; alternatively, she or he may struggle on, being ineffectual or even obstructing others in achieving joint goals. This is a great tragedy. For this reason, burnout — its recognition, causes, prevention and cures — needs to be taken seriously.

SYMPTOMS OF BURNOUT

Burning-out is a downward spiral. When we cut ourselves off from sources of nourishment, be they the natural environment, loved ones, or from inner spiritual sources of renewal and inspiration, the problems compound. We get more and more caught up in the delusion of separateness. Like a ring-barked tree, we are surrounded by nourishment but unable to let it in. We can lose the sense of wonder at what is still unspoilt in this world and the daily miracles before our eyes. In our quest for a better world, we may be failing to take action on the one thing we can really do something about — our own lives.

"I just felt like I was trying to run on 'Empty'."

One of the many physical signs of burnout is chronic fatigue: bone weariness that sleep does not dispel. People become vulnerable to diseases or find they cannot throw off minor illnesses such as colds. Other symptoms are frequent headaches, stomach pains and backache. Sleep patterns are often affected: some people have trouble getting to sleep, others wake in the early hours with their thoughts racing. High stress levels may lead to weight loss, or conversely to gain from overeating. Sex may seem like too much trouble. Some people increase their use of tobacco, marijuana, alcohol or tranquilizers as an escape. As one sufferer put it, "I just felt like I was trying to run on 'Empty'."

The emotional and mental effects can be even more distressing — for some it amounts to a personality change. Common feelings are depression, chronic anxiety and a sense of being overwhelmed or besieged by demands. Ideas of entrapment are frequent, compounded by an inability to perceive other options. Hair-trigger emotions can quickly produce tears or flare-ups.

Colleagues may notice withdrawal into isolation, rigid thinking, cynicism and negativity in someone who had formerly been quite positive. Previously well balanced people may evidence distorted perceptions of reality, such as paranoia — thinking that others are against them. These sorts of reactions inevitably lead to relationship and family problems, all of which add to the overall stress.

Burnout is qualitatively different from an acute stress reaction caused by a sudden crisis or a short burst of overwork. The effects are usually deeper. It is also a spiritual crisis. Bewildered sufferers may find themselves beset by a sense of futility; their life may be devoid of joy, they may

resent others and crave isolation from something that once seemed important and attractive. They are likely to be ambivalent, caught between wanting to escape from the situation on one hand, and obsession with keeping on going, on the other.

A client described to me: "I felt pretty guilty, and even embarrassed for going on like this but I just couldn't scrape up the energy to do something about it. I didn't want to admit it had become that bad — I'm usually so nice. It wasn't till I hit the bottom that I really got the message."

Burnout is kindled by taking on too much, too intensely, for too long. But it is not that simple. There is usually a complex web of causes that includes personal or internal factors, structural or organizational factors and societal factors such as social injustice. Ultimately, however, it is the way in which an individual interprets or reacts to these factors which makes the difference.

Humans are capable of sustained hard work under very difficult conditions without showing signs of burnout. This is demonstrated by third world peasants who often toil from dawn to dusk under impossible conditions; or people who put in superhuman efforts during wartime or emergencies. They may suffer exhaustion, but not necessarily burnout. So what sorts of things make that difference?

CAUSES OF BURNOUT

MOTIVES AND SENSE OF IDENTITY

Ram Dass and Paul Gorman wrote in *How Can I Help?*[1]

"It is not always our efforts that burn us out, it is where the mind is standing in relation to them." We may observe that the seeds of burnout are sown in how we enter into the helping act and in what we bring with us — particularly the models we have of ourselves. "Along with our clean shirt, good intentions and eagerness to serve, we've carried to work a number of needs and expectations. Sometimes burnout is simply our motives coming home to roost."

Social action is primarily motivated by idealistic values which can be very challenging to maintain in the face of a blatantly less-than-ideal world.

"The hotter the fire the better it burns; the more fiery the ambition, however, the greater the danger that the worker may burn out. Burnout is an occupational hazard for high achievers with high ideals."[2]

Our sense of identity or basic "OKness" can get excessively bound up in our work. Who we are can become equated with what we get done: "I can't be all bad if I do some good." When the problems we are tackling seem insurmountable and therefore don't get resolved quickly, self esteem can be badly eroded; or, driven by insecurity, we may set

PERSONAL FACTORS AS CAUSES OF BURNOUT

"Burnout is an occupational hazard for high achievers with high ideals." — Patricia Vizderman

up a situation to "prove" we are the only ones who can do the job properly. This excessive control may lead to a refusal to delegate or to an insistence on involvement in each stage of a project — with inevitable overload.

As we discussed in Chapter 4, "Insight as a Resource", our drive to change the "outer world" can be a reflection of an inner unresolved issue in our own life. I am not implying that we need to resolve the personal dimension to be authentically concerned for the world. However, awareness of these links will lessen potential distortions or the tendency to get obsessed. The fact that we realize an issue does have a personal dimension can be used to enrich our work.

OVEREXPOSURE AND OBSESSION

"Classical environmentalism has bred a peculiar negative political malaise among its adherents. Alerted to fresh horrors almost daily, they research the extent of the new life threatening situation, rush to protest it, and campaign exhaustively to prevent a future occurrence. It's a valuable service of course, but imagine a hospital that consists of only an emergency room. No maternity care, no pediatric clinic, no promising therapy; just mangled trauma cases. Many of them are lost or drag on in wilting protraction, and if a few are saved, there are always more than can be handled jamming through the door. Rescuing the environment has become like running a battlefield aid station against the killing machine that operates just beyond reach and shifts its ground after each seeming defeat."[3]

Do you believe that if you just work a little harder it will stem the flood of demands? Do you put life on hold until everything is cleared up? Unfortunately in most cases the demands are endless. Even more effort at trying harder will never be enough.

The first stage in a stress reaction is the release of adrenalin, which gives temporary bursts of energy and even induces euphoria. It is possible to become addicted to this. By continually pushing themselves harder the adrenalin addict can stay stimulated, firing on all cylinders much of the time. Unfortunately this cannot last indefinitely. The next stage is running out of fuel. Depression, lethargy and lack of direction is the end result.

Do you put life on hold until everything is cleaned up?

Similarly we can become hooked on bad news. Do you hunt out new information to keep you and those around you in a panic, or in a constant state of negativity? Our negative slant may result in bulletins that say " Here is another bit of bad news — you should be really outraged about this!" Or it can flourish in endless "ain't it awful" sessions.

EMOTIONAL ACCUMULATION

Even if we are not obsessively seeking out bad news, as people concerned about social issues we are more exposed to distressing realities. This awareness can be profoundly disturbing to a positive outlook on life and positive visions for the future. Feelings of grief, hopelessness, or despair may alternate with anger or even numbness and disbelief.

From time to time acknowledging the painful feelings and releasing them with support from others, often renews hope and energy. Finding out that others also care, brings us back to a simple vulnerability of being alive together in these daunting times. This process affirms the basic truth of our interconnectedness. Solutions will be woven out of our strength together rather than as separate, closed individuals. It is not merely a process of cathartic release. The issues still remain. But to share, validate and realize the power of our interconnectedness, while daring to speak our hopes and visions, keeps us from sinking into cynicism.

DENIAL OF PERSONAL NEEDS

As William Bryan, Director of the Northern Rockies Action Group, puts it:

"We just assume that the mission is more important than our personal needs. This is where a fundamental contradiction sets in. Those of us who are burnout-prone are also sensitive people who have feelings, want to be liked and recognized, and wish to do worthwhile things for other people. We want to do well and look good in the eyes of our peers, but unfortunately our peers are usually in the same dilemma. They also play down personal needs. Consequently, we fall into playing their game which is ours as well. This usually means that competition thrives between us... Who worked more hours last week? Who originated the better idea?... Purity tests abound as to who is the better environmentalist, feminist, civil rights advocate or socialist."[4]

Continuously pushing along and being strictly focussed on the task at hand is often a denial of our physical body and its basic needs. Missing exercise is a common habit, but this is just what's needed to cope with the stress. Aerobic exercise such as running, swimming or even brisk walking burns up the toxins produced by stress and contributes to relaxation. But there never seems to be enough time for that...

Include yourself as a valid environmental concern!

We may go further by ignoring messages from our bodies that we are tired and need a break (even to go to the toilet). How often do the cigarettes, sugar and coffee come out to override these messages to keep us going! If this becomes habitual our body has to resort to something more dramatic or painful to gain our attention.

Meals eaten tensely, on the run, are not digested properly. Takeaway foods are often not nutritious. Getting your nourishment this way eventually leads to health problems.

Evonne Rand is hard hitting:

"I am struck repeatedly by the degree to which people who are committed to 'good work' to making this world better to live in, do not include themselves as valid environmental concerns — not only at the level of potential burnout but also at the level of credibility. If you are saving the world and killing yourself (even passively by self-neglect) you will not be effective in your work. The people who you are trying to convince will not believe you. You can't abuse yourself and advocate that society not abuse the environment. It's a fundamental contradiction in terms — a good case of the old 'do as I say not as I do'.[5]

SELF NURTURING

Nurturing means, in the most simple sense, to attend to basic requirements: nourishing food, quality sleep, pleasant exercise and fresh air. However, taking care of ourselves extends well beyond this. Dealing with projects, people, and challenges on a daily basis (especially if it is done under pressure, with uncertainty and few external rewards) slowly drains our inner reserves. One way to "top up" again is to nurture ourselves, perhaps by little treats and pleasures, deep relaxation exercises, or meditation. Whatever renews and sustains one person may not do so for another. For some, renewal comes from a trip to the beach, a good novel, a sauna, or just wasting time on the veranda! As they say — whatever turns you on. Take the time to identify what the most valuable things are for you. (See What revives me p 130.)

When we are caught up in "Important Work" often self nurturing comes to be perceived as selfish or trivial; but it is these little treats and believing we are deserving of them, which can go a long way towards keeping on keeping on.

SUPPORT STRUCTURES

Support can come in many forms: from a luncheon meeting or a phone call to a more structured situation such as a formal support group. (See Chapter 10, "Support and Accountability Groups" and Chapter 8, "Working Together".) What is the quality of your conversations with people regarding your work? Is the nature of all interactions superficial and "doing" oriented?

Having the opportunity to reflect on your work with quality attention will aid in keeping things in balance. Take the time to review personal objectives, to realize what is working, celebrate what is going well, acknowledge difficulties and look for solutions. It is good to pay attention to the *how* rather than just the *what*. This sort of support is qualitatively different from informal discussions with co-workers which often lead to even more projects, requiring more effort...

Many activists can end up leading very unbalanced lives and may not notice until it is too late. One of the dilemmas of being committed to basic social change is that it touches all levels of our being. Involvement is not something that one can neatly close the door on at 5 pm. In fact for a lot of activists it might be a case of literally opening the door to the home-cum-office-cum- action headquarters: papers on the bed, meetings round the kitchen table... Operating in this way means there's no getting away from it! **INFRINGEMENT INTO PERSONAL LIFE**

Though all this activity has the potential to enrich our lives, it is this feature of unceasing demands which creates much fuel for burnout. It also leads to deterioration of relationships. After-hours phone calls, night organizing of meetings, weekend activities and work-related visitors infringe on the time with children or partners. Parties become just another venue to talk shop ("networking").

Do you, for instance, use your holidays as an opportunity for catching up on your workload or reading? Often families of activists are expected not only to make considerable financial sacrifices but also to forgo quality contact with each other because the immediate needs of "the cause" are more pressing.

There are many useful tools to keep control of workloads. Techniques such as timelines make it clear when things need to start and the critical points which need to be reached in order to finish on time. Time can be parcelled so it reflects priorities. Using such methods it is easier, for instance, to avoid things such as spending days organizing a demo (if it is not likely to get much attention) while direct personal lobbying of the power brokers is neglected. A simple guide for over expansion is to "Do less and do it better". A support group can help to organize these simple time management structures. **PERSONAL PLANNING AND TIME MANAGEMENT**

Use the organization's operating plan as a guide to priority areas and personal planning will flow on accordingly. Remember to integrate important events, holidays, opportunities for learning, and formulate a clear idea of what your limits are. (See weekly organizer sheet, p 136.)

If you find you are perpetually too busy to do this level of planning, you must ask yourself who is actually in control of your life?

It is important to develop some objectivity about your work style, so you can remove counter-productive patterns — such as needing an imminent deadline to start producing. Explore ways to optimize your potential. **WORK STYLE**

For Peter, the mornings are when inspiration flows, for me the late night hours are the best. I need a long warm-up to a task with uninterrupted periods. Pat needs a lot of variety and people contact. Communicate these sorts of preferences to others, so there is less likelihood of misunderstanding. Do you do your best work doing when handling several things at once or when you can focus on one thing at a time?

TIME OUT A basic anti-burnout strategy is to be able to take time off (as opposed to pseudo time off when you catch up on your work!). Take time off at the end of each day, each week, or take short breaks after intense bursts; and have a genuine annual holiday. That might require making agreements not to talk shop with colleagues,and having time when you're not "on call". Remember, the telephone does not always have to be answered. The concept of taking "sabbaticals" provides an opportunity for having some extended time away to rethink, renew and rest, without having to resign or burn out to do it.

The transition between being "on" and "off" may be important. Christina Maslach in her book *Burnout, the High Cost of Caring*[6] uses the useful analogy of "decompression" time between working and nonworking times, that allows you to unwind and leave the job behind. For many it is an activity which is in sharp contrast to their typical work routine. Perhaps you want solitude, or to be very physical or to engage in something totally "unmeaningful".

Research into "peak performers" (people who excel in their chosen field) by Charles Garfield showed that nearly all of them were quite devoted to hobbies unrelated to their main area.

Time off is important for nurturing or initiating primary relationships. Also, building friendship and community networks are as important in creating a better world as the more overtly political work that we may engage in.

CRITICISM Another source of stress may be the fear of reprisal or criticism. It is often a reality for people engaged in controversial issues. There may be fear of physical harm — for one's self or family, social ostracism, or criticism for not meeting society's or your family's particular expectations.

Expectations such as pursuing recognized careers, earning better money, or generally being more "normal" exert pressure on us. Bob described it: "Somehow I'd managed to ignore all the little jabs I'd been getting from the family and neighbors. But when I started to get exhausted and it just wasn't so clear cut any more, they got through my skin. I started to doubt everything." This is where a support group or community can be extremely valuable: to provide some perspective, affirm the courage of your stand, or even arrange some protection.

However, for many of us the main source of corrosive criticism is internalized. In our continuous inner dialogue, there is a "voice" that gives us a hard time. It is a judgmental or parental part of our psyche. This part can be pretty difficult to please. Bringing this "self talk" into conscious awareness, and examining the rationality of its contents, will free us up to act in more life enhancing ways. (See the critic shrinking exercise, p 19.)

Such techniques as Voice Dialogue, Transactional Analysis, Gestalt, and Psychodrama, indepth journal writing or meditation, will develop insight into these personal dynamics. (Most bookshops have a personal growth section with self help books on these topics or look at noticeboards for practitioners or groups who provide these types of opportunities.) While we may not entirely silence the inner dialogue, we can "reprogram" it to be more affirming and accepting. If we see clearly the roots of the endless striving, and the constant battle to maintain our self esteem, burnout will be minimized.

ROLE MODELS

One of the problems of trying to feel "good enough" is that sometimes the role models for effective activists are based on standards set by fanatical workaholics, or at least by people who have exceptional abilities to withstand stress. William Bryan describes this as the "Ralph Nader Syndrome", named after the legendary crusader for consumer rights in the late sixties who led a monastic lifestyle and worked phenomenal hours. Bryan claims few people are actually capable of keeping up this kind of pace, although we often judge ourselves and each other by these standards and thus set ourselves up for a sense of failure.

Feeling insecure can lead to "doing more and more for longer and longer".

We need to check whether these seemingly admirable people do have a healthy work style. Perhaps they are one of the relatively rare racehorses who have exceptional ability to withstand stress. Or perhaps we don't see the whole story — the effects on their personal life or their health. Perhaps they are unwittingly on the road to burnout. We should look instead for role models of people who are effective but who also joyfully sustain themselves. (See exercise on Identifying role models, p 131.) Ask yourself whether you are aiming to be extraordinary in your work or are prepared to be more ordinary and relatively happy and healthy.

FEEDBACK

If you are feeling so insecure that you need to do more and more for longer and longer, you may be only making the assumption that you are not meeting others' expectations — whether it is the committee, co-workers, funding bodies, or parents. The most direct way to work out the reality is by asking for feedback.

Some years ago I was working as a coordinator of the local Neighborhood Center. I took on more and more community development projects — just about anything that anybody suggested, plus any I could think of. We expanded the staff and extended the building rapidly and went through quite a bit of upheaval in the process. I was plagued by feelings of inadequacy, of not making a big enough difference. Inevitably I became overwhelmed, exhausted, and then I quit.

I failed to directly ask the staff or the management committee for feedback on my work, or for their actual expectations, nor was this feedback offered. From my contact with them later on, I gleaned they would have preferred me to slow down, stop generating "so damn many projects" — even if they were good ideas — and be more available for informal contact. It was a lesson.

One structure for getting feedback in a positive and constructive way is using the "clearness process".[7] (See Consultancy or Clearness Meetings, p 113.)

WHEN ALL ELSE FAILS WE CAN ALWAYS LAUGH

Let's challenge joylessness! Create opportunities to play at work and at home, in an innocent, spontaneous way. Doing this will recontact the inner child. This natural child part has enormous reserves of energy, joy and a great ability to bounce back. How often in the seriousness of saving the world does this aspect of ourselves get neglected! You may retort "How can I laugh when the issues I am facing are definitely not funny?". However, Ram Dass and Paul Gorman[8] point out that when facing apparently hopeless situations, we are living in the land of Catch 22:

"The challenge is to turn it into M*A*S*H*. Here we are in the service, with a crazy war going on all around, no idea when it will end, stuck every day with the same fellow idiots. Still we have to find some way to stay conscious. We'd better. Wounded people are coming in from out of the sky and they're screaming. ... when we're hard on the job it's the one-pointed concentration of the surgeon... and the rest of the time we throw a party. We take in every absurd, contradictory, counterproductive aspect of the war zone and transform it into grist for irony, humor, irreverence and creative mischief. That's how we stay nimble inside."

Although we need to know that what we pour our hearts and minds into is effective, at some point letting go of the results is also called for to enable us to continue sanely. "We do what we can. Yet we cannot presume to know the final meaning of our actions. We cannot help but see them against a larger backdrop in which the ultimate significance of a single life may not be clear. We often cannot be in a position to perceive the cumulative effect of individual actions."[9]

LETTING GO OF RESULTS AND CULTIVATING PERSPECTIVE

In this line of work there is no place for excessive attachment to results. Fran Peavey taught us to chant with great vigor and clenched-fist salutes "The people united sometimes win and sometimes lose!"

EXERCISES

Burnout Rating Scale

Think over the past 3 months and answer the following questions according to how often you have experienced these symptoms.

0 = Never
1 = Very rarely
2 = Rarely
3 = Sometimes
4 = Often
5 = Very often

Adding up your total score will give you some indication whether you are likely to burn out or not.

1. Do you feel fatigued in a way that rest or sleep does not relieve?
2. Do you feel more cynical, pessimistic or disillusioned about things you used to feel positive about?
3. Do you feel a sadness or an emptiness inside?
4. Do you have physical symptoms of stress, eg. insomnia, stomach pains, headaches, migraines?
5. Is your memory unreliable?
6. Are you irritable or emotional with a short fuse?
7. Have you been more susceptible to illness lately, eg. colds, 'flu, food allergies, hay fever?
8. Do you feel like isolating yourself from colleagues, friends or family?
9. Is it hard to enjoy yourself, have fun, relax and experience joy in your life?
10. Do you feel that you are accomplishing less in your work?

SCORING 0 –15 You are doing well.
16–25 Some attention needed, you may be a candidate.
26–35 You are on the road to burnout.
Make changes now.
36–50 You need to take action immediately — your health and well-being are threatened.

What revives me The purpose of this exercise is to identify things — activities, practises, responses — which nourish your inner being and revive you, and to extend your range. This exercise also helps to discourage patterns of self denial.

- **Individually, or in small groups, brainstorm things that you find revive you, keep you sane under pressure and contribute to staying in touch with yourself.**

- **Review: Which ones take little time or money? Which ones take solitude? Which ones need to be done with others?**

- **In pairs or small groups discuss the ones you do now and those you will/could do in future.**

If the above is done as a group exercise, the leader should encourage expressions of creativity, promote an atmosphere of respect, and emphasize the value of pleasurable things. Highlight the diversity.

This exercise can also be based on the theme of "What gives me pleasure?"

Create a retreat space The purpose of this exercise is to create an imaginary place of escape and rest to use (in your imagination) whenever needed. The exercise can be extended to stimulate ideas and commitment for creating an actual private retreat place.

- Start with a brief relaxation exercise.

- Give yourself a few minutes to imagine your perfect retreat. Where is it? Perhaps on a deserted island, a four poster bed with the curtains drawn, a tent in the wilderness ... What are the surroundings like? The sounds? The smells? The textures? What might you have with you? Make it as vivid as you can... This imaginary place is available to you whenever you need to relieve stress and it only takes a moment to get there.

- Share the image with a partner for a few minutes or make a painting of what you saw.

- How could you create a real life retreat place? It could be a seat in the garden, a tree house, a bath by candlelight, a table in the local library or cafe, or a secret walk. Is it possible to set aside a room or a corner in your house which is a "Breathing Space" — for quiet reflection or meditation? Decorate it in soothing colors and textures, perhaps with images that are calming or meaningful to you. Add a few soft cushions, perhaps a candle or lamp. Enjoy creating a special place.

The purpose of this exercise is to clarify who your role models are, and assess whether aspiring to be like them is healthy for you. It can be done alone or in groups of 2–3, taking it in turns to be the focus person. Partners ask questions and help to assess the effect these role models have. Take about 10–15 minutes each.

Identifying role models

- Close your eyes, relax deeply and let images arise of the people who have been role models for you. Who have you really wanted to be like — particularly in your work for social change?

- Draw a quick picture or write their names on bits of paper, then place these on the floor in different locations in the room.

- Go to stand on each spot and talk as if you were that person. How would s/he stand? Let yourself be the person for a time and ask: What are my good qualities and strengths? What are my weaknesses? What are other aspects of my life like? Is it lonely, exhausting? Do I know when to stop? How am I likely to end up? Continue doing this for each person you identified as important.

- Step back into being yourself and evaluate: How is having these people as role models stress-creating for me? Is it healthy for me to aspire to be like them? What needs modifying? In what ways is it unrealistic for me and my circumstances?

The purpose of this exercise is to identify things which make the transition from focussed work time to private or family time easier. Often when we are stressed, we neglect to make this transition, and the omission can lead to arguments, resentment and extra pressure.

Decompression activities

The exercise can be done as a personal compilation (even as a poem), or by talking in pairs, or as a group brainstorm.

1. What things help you to leave work behind, unwind and prepare yourself for a different part of your life?

2. What things do you do (or not do) presently which impede your making this transition?

3. What are some other possibilities that you haven't tried?

4. What will you make a commitment to yourself to do in the next week?

"Get off my back!" This is a bioenergetics exercise which lifts your energy level and also raises awareness of burdens you may be carrying. It is fun to do in a group, and can be a good break in meetings.

- Slump forward in a chair as if you were carrying a heavy burden. Visualize what you might be carrying currently in your life (or from the past): perhaps responsibilities, guilt, unfinished projects etc.

- Now leap up and vigorously thrust your elbows backwards with clenched fists while yelling out: "Get off my back!" Continue this for a few minutes till you have loosened your load. Then have a general shake out of your arms and legs to relax them.

- Sit and breathe quietly while you reflect on your experience for a few minutes.

Web chart for identifying stressors The purpose of this exercise is to raise your awareness of things which are contributing to stress. You will need large sheets of paper and a few different colored pens.

- **Start with the word STRESS and put a circle around it, in the middle of the sheet of paper. Then quickly and without censoring, draw lines and bubbles with things that have lately been contributing to stress in your life. Start with the major ones or direct causes. Then flow on out to the more indirect causes. Draw lines to link ones which go together.**

- **Now go through and color in the ones you can do something about. Perhaps color code them; for instance, the more serious ones in red, less serious ones in pink etc. With which stresses do you need**

Your web chart may look something like this:

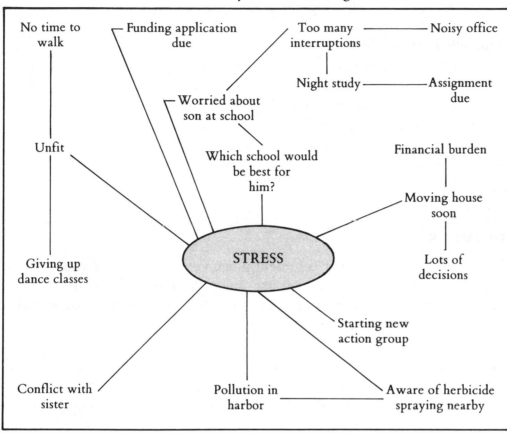

some help or cooperation to change? What steps can you take to lessening these factors in the next week? The next month?

A variation on this exercise, or a follow on, is to do the exercise in positive terms with WHOLENESS/ FEELING GOOD in the middle. Then draw a web of the things which contribute to that state in your life.

This exercise can be done alone or in pairs, taking it in turns to listen to one another.

Setting limits

1. What are the easiest things for you to say *no* to?
2. What are the hardest things for you to say *no* to?
3. What effect does it have on you when you won't say *no?*
4. What do you intend doing about this? Who could assist you?

Now take some time to practice saying No! to the things you have identified in question 2, with your partner trying to wheedle and persuade you to say yes.

If you recognize that this is a difficult area for you, you could consider doing an assertiveness training class, or seek some personal therapy work around the issue of boundaries. It might make a big difference to the effectiveness of your work and your ability to avoid burnout.

Identifying your inner "drivers"

The purpose of this exercise is to identify what beliefs and internal statements we may be adhering to, which we use to drive ourselves hard. Though these "drivers" seem to be socially desirable superficially, to feel compelled internally to obey them can severely limit our ability to take good care of ourselves, to enjoy what we do and to succeed in our goals. The internal sense of a driver is "If I do this thing enough, I will get approval". These statements and beliefs are learnt in early childhood and become habits of living unless we consciously change them.

The notion of drivers used in this exercise is derived from Transactional Analysis, based on the work of Taibi Kahler and others.

DRIVERS

"Hurry Up" — This driver is present when you continually hassle yourself about time. Whatever it is you are doing, you feel like you should be doing it faster, leading to panic about not having enough time. It makes it hard to do anything in a relaxed way.

"Be Strong" — This driver tells you: "Don't show your feelings." "Don't ask for help, be the one to take on the responsibility." Such a message makes it hard to be vulnerable. Men especially are taught this one.

"Be Perfect" — This driver demands that you Be Good at Everything even if you're a beginner; don't make mistakes, and strive constantly to perfect yourself.

"Be Pleasing" — Try above all to meet other people's needs rather than your own. Do not show your displeasure, avoid conflict and smile even if you don't feel like it. Women especially are taught this one.

"Try Hard" — Engage in a lot of effort in what you do; put the emphasis on being seen to be trying, rather than succeeding. You tend to run around in circles a lot.

Do you recognize any of these as the way you behave?

It is useful to make a subjective assessment of the relative strength of each of these internal drivers for you, in order to understand where you need to pay particular attention and do some personal work to loosen their grip on your life. Try rating their relative strength, as in the example below.

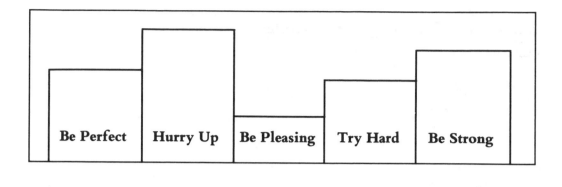

Be Perfect   Hurry Up   Be Pleasing   Try Hard   Be Strong

The next stage is to either ask yourself these questions or with a partner take it in turns to reflect on the following:

1. In what way do the ones you rated highly operate in your life?
2. What effect do they have on your work for social change?
3. How might they contribute to burnout?
4. Do you notice yourself giving these kinds of messages to your children or your work colleagues?

It seems to take sustained awareness to decrease driver behavior. When we are under particular stress, we are more likely to revert to it. Gaining objectivity gives us a choice.

5. What sort of "permissions" would you need to give yourself in order to counteract the old driver habit?

> eg. It is OK to do things at my pace.
> To err is human.
> Don't bother trying, just do it!
> It is OK to please *me.*
> Lots of people would love to help me.

Design just the right statements for yourself that you need to be reminded of, write them in big letters on paper, then stick them on the fridge door or the bathroom mirror. Tell your friends and/or your support groups how you intend to change these things. Ask people to remind you when

Weekly organizer worksheet

WEEK BEGINNING: ....

DONE ✓	WHAT	WHO TO CONTACT	WHEN BY
☐ ☐ ☐ ☐ ☐	**WORK/SOCIAL ACTION**	....	....
☐ ☐ ☐ ☐ ☐	**PERSONAL/FAMILY**	....	....
☐ ☐ ☐ ☐	**SELF CARE/FUN/RELAXATION**	....	....
☐ ☐ ☐ ☐	**OTHER**	....	....
☐ ☐ ☐	**HOLD FOR LATER**	....	....
☐ ☐	**RUBBISH BIN**	....	....

they notice you getting into them again. Make a note in your diary to compare yourself in 6 months time.

NOTES

1. Ram Dass & Paul Gorman, *How Can I Help?* Alfred A. Knopf, New York, 1986.

2. Patricia Vigderman, *New Age Magazine*, Summer, 1985.

3. Peter Berg quoted by Ann Herbert in "Let the Good Times Last", *Awakening In The Nuclear Age Journal*, No 6, 1985.

4. Dr. William L. Bryan, *Preventing Burnout In The Public Interest Community*, Northern Rockies Action Group Paper Volume 3, No 3. 1980. NRAG, Helena, Montana. I am indebted to him for inspiration on sections of this and the next chapter.

5. Evonne Rand in Bryan, *Preventing Burnout* ...

6. Cristina Maslach *"Burnout — The Cost Of Caring"*, Spectrum Books, Prentice Hall, 1982.

7. Peter Woodrow, "Clearness Process for Supporting Individuals and Groups in Decision Making," New Society Publishers, Philadelphia.

8. Ram Dass & Gorman, *How Can I Help?*

9. *Ibid.*

PREVIOUS PAGE
USE COLORED PENS TO MARK HIGH PRIORITIES.
IF THESE CATEGORIES DO NOT FIT — RENAME THEM.
PHOTOCOPY THIS SHEET AND FILL IN WEEKLY TO KEEP
THINGS IN PERSPECTIVE.

CHAPTER TWELVE

Building Fireproof Organizations

Good conditions include an atmosphere where it is OK to have fun!

Often the discussion of stress and burnout is limited to the individual context, as if they required just private personal solutions. Yet the way we run organizations, and the intrinsic stresses that get passed on to workers, has a significant impact on whether workers end up burning out or not. Some groups are burnout prone, despite the good intentions, enthusiasm and dedication of individuals in these organizations — people just don't last. Burnout may spread like wildfire through these organizations, particularly if the key decision-makers are cynical, defensive or blocking creative problem-solving. This can happen to both voluntary and paid workers.

Fortunately the same factors which contribute to burnout-proofing an organization also contribute to increased effectiveness and foster more enjoyable, cohesive groups. Burnout-proofing your group may lie in such things as improved planning and building a group ethos that values the importance of individual needs. Paying attention to the group's process as well as the content is crucial, as is keeping an eye on creeping rigidity in ideologies which may be oppressive. Good conditions include an atmosphere where it is OK to have fun!

GOOD PLANNING

Ironically an organization whose aim is to promote a tacky consumer product such as plastic war toys may have better resources, clearer goals and more efficient methods of reaching them than a group aiming to promote world peace.

CLEAR GOALS AND PRIORITIES

Many social action groups know what they don't want but might find it difficult to articulate what they do want and how they can measure it when they have it. Aspirations might be expressed in lofty terms like "elimination of nuclear weapons", "total equality for women" and so on. Because these may not actually be achievable in the short term, one could be up against a nebulous feeling of continuous failure. Success is elusive. It may take generations to reach these goals.

Long term goals can be broken down into clear and realistic medium and short term objectives. Then agreement can be reached on priorities, which provides clarity and a basis for strategy or action plans. Operating in this way lessens stressful pressure and most importantly gives the individual worker some structure for setting limits. Without clear goals it is so easy for a group to get sidetracked and fragmented; to stay on the treadmill of responding to endless so-called "great opportunities" or "great disasters".

Panic leads to crisis improvisation, repeated work, foul-ups, and doing things by halves. Campaigns often break down because they are set up to happen too fast due to some perceived urgent need based on what the opposition is doing. That is what sports people call "playing the other team's game".

Following a hierarchy of planning is the basis for qualitative, systematic change. This may seem so obvious it is overlooked. A failure to do this level of planning may be attributed to naivete or in some cases, the apparent urgency. "Who's got time to stop and just sit around talking?" is a common rebuttal. As we discussed in Chapter 9, rebelliousness may be a factor: "These rational, linear tools belong to the capitalist/ patriarchal system, and we don't want to know about operating like that." Do we settle instead for the tyranny of structurelessness?

CLEAR EXPECTATIONS

If an organization doesn't have clear goals and priorities it is hard for an individual worker (which includes volunteers) to develop them. Ambiguity of role or role conflict is a major contributing factor to burnout. A group member will experience a pull between mixed accountabilities. For instance:

One environment group received funding to run some programs for school children on the importance of trees, but the committee really wanted to spend the money on purchasing bulk seedlings and equipment. The coordinator and some of the volunteers thought information booklets for adults, on tree planting in the local area, was what was most needed.

"I ended up feeling like the proverbial meat in the sandwich," remarked the coordinator. "Doing a little bit of each of these projects meant that didn't end up having much effect."

Anything which clarifies what is expected from each worker is well worth the effort. Most business or professional roles have written job descriptions. How many jobs in the social action field have clear job specifications? Just because it is a voluntary or low paid position does

A person in an ambiguous role can end up feeling like the proverbial meat in the sandwich.

not lessen the need. Job descriptions are useful when they are realistic and cover the sorts of things that actually happen, including fundraising, answering enquiries, selling merchandise, or billeting out-of-town colleagues. These descriptions need to be reviewed periodically. If new demands arise, the question to ask is:

"What has to go to make room for this?"

Avoid at all cost the question,

"Where do I/we cram this new bit in?"

Too much or too little autonomy can be a major stress factor for workers in organizations. People have different needs according to their levels of skills and experience, personality type and actual demands of the job. Similarly the amount and quality of supervision a person receives may play a significant role in her/his ability to perform the job well and to feel at ease with it.

The organization has some responsibility to protect individual workers from undue outside pressure. Sensitivity is required to notice, for instance, that some individuals are being drained by too many disruptions, by dealing with irate consumers or too many people wanting information endlessly. It may require a group restructuring to offer them more protection. One example is making it policy to put the answering machine on during meetings.

The receptionist at my counseling center initially had to find replacements for her lunch break. This put her in the position of asking a favor from others, whereas a roster looked like a clear non-stressful solution. Nice idea — but it still didn't work because no one wanted to go on the roster and miss lunch. The resolution was the answering machine and a "come back later" sign. This illustrates the point that a series of restructurings is often necessary until everyone's needs are met.

In the life of a group there are particularly critical phases for restructuring. If the group or organization is in a phase of rapid expansion, (even though this might be seen as highly desirable), the extra demands will put the workers under added stress. Assimilating, orienting and training new people takes energy, as does adjusting to the new internal group dynamics. Existing structures often prove to be inadequate for new conditions. Chaos may ensue before new ones are established.

Contraction can also be stressful, especially if paid jobs are being lost. Funding cutbacks, lack of morale, or a shift in public consciousness, can limit the flow of new participants or voluntary workers. This is likely to lower morale futher and encourage tired workers to "soldier on". People in this position may feel they have to choose between the demise of the the project or their own demise. A group strategy review is called for at this point, before the burnout embers flare.

If your group's objectives are clear, and stated in such a way that it is obvious when they are achieved, it is much easier to evaluate your effectiveness. Good times to stop and reflect on these things are: at the end of a phase in a campaign, after a major project, or before gearing up for something new. The goals themselves should be reviewed periodically with such questions as:

REGULAR REVIEW AND EVALUATION

Are these still our priorities?
Have the circumstances changed?
Are there unresolved conflicts still lingering?
What has been learnt so far?

Review and evaluation can be done on a group and individual basis. For individuals, the peer review or performance appraisal systems followed by some professional groups is just as appropriate for the community based activist in a cohesive group. The system involves checking-in with the job description, current goals and projects, and encouraging the staff member or voluntary worker to raise issues or make changes as needed. Review times are also a great opportunity for positive feedback — don't assume we all know when we are doing a good job! Especially if burnout has started to set in, people are more likely to assume that lack of feedback implies criticism. Review meetings can offer stimulation, validation and encouragement as well as ironing out difficulties.

Group victory celebrations, when goals are reached, are tremendously valuable. Brisbane People For Nuclear Disarmament put on a public picnic in the park to celebrate the signing of the US–Soviet arms limitation agreement in 1987. As one participant put it: "It gave me a lift to have a celebration for a change. I had been doing so much protesting. It also let me share in the feeling that we all made a difference... my drops were part of the turning of the tide."

"It gave me a lift to have a celebration for a change. I had been doing so much protesting."

The sense of panic and obsession, and patterns of driving oneself, that were discussed earlier in an individual context, can also easily become the group ethos. In this atmosphere the denial of personal needs is projected onto others as an expectation. Perhaps you have experienced being part of a group where you got the covert message — "It is definitely not OK to look relaxed, or as if you are enjoying yourself." This message is implying you are not serious enough about the issue or committed enough — or even suffering enough!

William Bryan, who was a Coordinator of the Northern Rockies Action Group, suggests that there is "a common and fundamentally flawed belief

VALUING THE INDIVIDUAL

in social change work that the self is unimportant. There is the illusion that the cause is everything. And when an activist deviates from that belief, he/she is then accused by his/her peers of being narcissistic and of taking the easy road. Paranoia sets in, with the well-intentioned activist fearful of getting low marks on a social change purity test conducted by fellow activists!"[1] Can you identify with any of this in your work team?

As was stressed in the "Working Together" chapter, a shift in emphasis is required to encompass process as well as content or task. Being aware of process means looking at not only what tasks are getting done, but how they are being done, and what effect this is having on participants. If burnout is to be prevented we not only need encouragement to be inwardly focussed at times, but also that we can do so without any implication that we "should feel guilty". Our aims for building a better, safer, less exploitative world must be congruent with our process. Without this, where is the integrity, or even hope of long-term success?

Carolyn Cotton, an anti-nuclear activist, said: "We get so caught up in time-limited objectives that we forget to consider how carefully, how lovingly we are doing our work. We can also forget to consider that most change happens not in 'event' but in one-to-one relationships. A large part of lobbying, for instance, isn't changing minds, it's just building friendships."[2]

MEETINGS How long is it since you went to a meeting that was enjoyable as well as effective? Meetings that start late, go overtime and are frustrating due to inadequate facilitation, will add a lot of fuel to the burnout pyre. Unclear processes for resolving conflicts and lack of meeting structure which leads to overload or confusion, also waste a lot of energy and breeds discontent. (See Chapter 9 for suggestions.)

The Movement for a New Society, which formed groups of committed social activists throughout the USA, from the 60's to mid 80's, particularly in Philadelphia, consolidated and articulated many useful process skills for social change movements. Their publications through New Society Publishers were the fruition of much experimentation and a sincere search for integrity in building true social change.

Inviting people with good group process and evaluation skills to participate on committees, in support groups, or to facilitate periodic staff development sessions, can provide this input and develop skills within the group, especially before crisis points are reached. From the work my colleagues and I have done with many groups, we have found the anti-burnout workshops/playshops or other team building processes, to be invaluable. They offer an opportunity for groups to explore issues of working together which need attention. By creating this oasis participants enjoy each other in a new way and the spirit of the group is renewed.

Much radical social action is done, in Australia at least, by people who are paid nothing or very little. Many rely on social security payments as a source of meager income. If social activists are getting paid for their work, there is no justification for assuming it should be low. Low pay over a long time can put quite a strain on individuals and families. If workers can't be paid, or the pay is low, is it possible to set up other rewards for service? Perhaps through barter for food, providing transport or childcare, offering a caravan at the beach for some time off, or discounts for services. There are lots of possibilities.

RESOURCES AND WORK CONDITIONS

A "poverty mentality" can lead to enormous inefficiency and frustration.

The planning process should include some financial planning, so that resources, however meager, are used effectively. A low budget should not mean that everything is done on the smallest possible shoestring, and stretched as far as it will reach. This "poverty mentality" sometimes leads to enormous inefficiency and frustration, adding to the strain. The faulty borrowed equipment for the film showings, the screen printed posters that didn't work, the old manual typewriter with the keys that stick... I'm sure many a funny yarn could be told looking back, but!! It is better to do less with more quality — which supports the integrity of the participants. Doing less with higher efficiency and professionalism is also likely to attract more support from donors or volunteers.

Other work conditions, such as taking compensatory time off for night or weekend work, is important in maintaining personal well-being. This is sometimes discouraged by inferences from co-workers that it shows a lack of commitment or it is a luxury with stretched resources. These unstated group pressures feed into our own internal pressures or "drivers" (See Identifying your inner "drivers" p 134). For example if you have a pronounced internal "Be Strong" and the group ethos denies nourishment and self care, these compound each other.

How many of these social action jobs, if they do pay, have decent, "I'm-totally-unavailable" type, paid holidays? Sick leave is rarely OK to take before you are half-dead. Are there provisions for any long service or "sabbatical" leave, or don't we ever expect people to last that long? Such things as opportunity for advancement through a career structure, or long term security of employment are mostly non-existent.

Is there any way this can be compensated for? Providing training or personal development opportunities and temporary staff swaps with other relevant organizations are possible ways to enrich job satisfaction. Without these things, too many good people feel forced eventually to leave.

BEAUTY AND ORDER

Lack of resources can mean many social action groups are working under conditions that would put unionized labor out on strike. Going into the offices of groups I am often struck by the noise, clutter and general air of disorganization. Many times the office space is crowded and shared with another organization.

I sometimes wonder if the cluttered look is cultivated by some to add to an air of "important and urgent work". The thinking would be,"Beauty and order are the values of the bourgeois — we will have none of that here". Phones are buried under piles of papers needing attention, posters on the walls keep hammering home how desperate the situation is ... For the tidy people of this world and their sympathizers, just being in these sorts of conditions is enough to burn them out in a few months!

If you were the kind of person who could do your homework with rock 'n roll playing and your little brother building leggo on your desk, you might even thrive in these sorts of office conditions, but many people can't function.

> Questions to ask:
> Are there ways to reduce noise levels, clutter, heat, and flow-through interruptions? Is a beauty and order coordinator appropriate? Can a quiet work corner be created for contemplation or concentrated work?

CREATE AN ATMOSPHERE OF GOOD PRACTICES

Simple work habits have a lot to do with creating an atmosphere of centeredness, which is essential to good quality work and end products. How can other group members support changes in individuals who have bad personal patterns that could lead to burnout? It might be necessary to challenge any panic or busyness "rackets" — where you get the feeling you should feel guilty if you're not at least looking terribly busy, even when it is quiet.

Do you get the feeling that you should look terribly busy all the time, even when it's quiet?

Take a good look at the reasons behind continual panic about deadlines or the apparent need to put in extra time. Make agreements about interruptions and respecting "Do Not Disturb" times. And of course, observe the simple good habits of taking lunch hours and tea breaks, for which unions fought so hard. *Refrain from giving "gold stamps" to people who deny themselves these breaks.*

When we work with the whole in mind, we need to be reminded that: "Large change doesn't come from clever quick fixes from smart tense people, but from long conversations and silences among people who know different things and need to learn different things."[3]

Burnout is not inevitable. To sustain ourselves for the long haul we need to ensure that we are working together in situations where support, clarity, laughter and fun are sincerely viewed as virtues.

EXERCISES

The purpose of this exercise is to step back and evaluate your daily work experience and consider aspects that need to be improved to maintain your well-being.

Drawing Your Experience of Work

You will need large sheets of paper, some paints, colored pencils or crayons. It could also be done as a sculpture with clay or plasticine on a firm base.

- **Settle back and relax for a few minutes in silence with your eyes closed.**

- **Now let images start to float up of your typical work day, whether you get paid for it or not. What is it like at its best, what is it like at its worst?**

- **Draw, paint or sculpt the images that you are forming. Just let them flow uncensored.**

- **When you have finished, share your impressions with a partner. The main themes could be discussed in the larger group also.**

The purpose of this exercise is to formulate anti-burnout group strategies. Since it is likely to highlight a number of issues that will need attention, it would be appropriate to first outline the symptoms of burnout and the fact that there are usually individual and organizational factors which contribute to it. This exercise draws attention to the potential organizational factors for your group.

Fireproofing Your Organization

If the group is larger than 8, divide into smaller groups of 4–6.

Firstly generate ideas by doing 3 short brainstorms of 5 minutes each on the following 3 questions. There should be no discussion, comments or censure at this stage. Just put down all the phrases and ideas as people offer them.

- **How might the way this group operates be contributing towards burnout among our workers?**

- **What needs to be included in our group's anti-burnout strategy?**

- **What can we do as individuals or as a group when we perceive that a co-worker is on the path to burnout?**

When the 3 topics have been brainstormed, spend up to 10 minutes on each one discussing the ideas. From these formulate concise summaries and recommendations. There may be suggestions that not everyone agrees with; note the controversial ones on a separate list. A spokesperson then reads these summaries back to the larger group. (Preferably write them up so everyone can see them.)

Spend the next 30 minutes to 1 hour deciding on any policy decisions, planning and changes that will put your strategy into effect. Keep discussing the controversial items until either you reach a solution, or you make some plan to deal with them at another time.

Rating Scale — How Burnout Prone Is Your Organization?

1. *PLANNING & PROJECT MANAGEMENT*: How clear are your group's goals and priorities?

|⌐_____|_____|_____|_____|_____¬|

Very unclear   Well planned/clear

2. *EXPECTATIONS*: How clear is it to each worker (including volunteers) what is expected of her/him?

|⌐_____|_____|_____|_____|_____¬|

Very unclear/conflicting   Clear/congruent

3. *EVALUATION*: How often does your group evaluate what it has achieved?

|⌐_____|_____|_____|_____|_____¬|

Never   Very often

4. *CELEBRATING & ACKNOWLEDGING ACHIEVEMENTS*: How often does your group celebrate successes & achievements?

|⌐_____|_____|_____|_____|_____¬|

Never   Frequently

5. *INDIVIDUAL NEEDS*: How much value does your group put on individual needs and opportunities for development?

|⌐_____|_____|_____|_____|_____¬|

None   High priority

6. *PRESSURE, TENSION & URGENCY:* What is the overall pace and intensity like?

|_____|_____|_____|_____|

Unrelentingly urgent & intense   Relaxed, steady pace

7. *WORK CONDITIONS:* In general what are the resources (equipment, venue, wages) like for your group?

|_____|_____|_____|_____|

Poor   Very good

8. *GENERAL WORKING ATMOSPHERE:* What is the atmosphere in your workplace?

|_____|_____|_____|_____|

Chaotic/disorganized   Centered/organized

9. *AUTONOMY:* How satisfied are you with your level of autonomy in your work?

|_____|_____|_____|_____|

Very dissatisfied   Very satisfied

10. *SUPERVISION:* How satisified are you with the quality of supervision you receive?

|_____|_____|_____|_____|

Very dissatisfied   Very satisfied

11. *DEALING WITH CONFLICT:* How effective is your group at resolving conflict constructively?

|_____|_____|_____|_____|

Totally ineffective   Highly effective

NOTES
1. William Bryan, "Preventing Burnout in the Public Interest Community," The *NRAG Papers*, Vol 3, No 3, Fall, 1980. I am indebted to his ideas in writing this chapter.

2. Quoted in "Nuclear Times" Newsletter of New England Peace Coalition, 1986.

3. Ann Herbert, "Let the Good Times Last," in *Awakening In The Nuclear Age Journal* (Interhelp USA), Fall, 1986.

CHAPTER THIRTEEN
Rekindling

·-

"By yielding I endure The empty space is filled When I give of myself I become more When I feel most destroyed I am about to grow When I desire nothing, a great deal comes to me." — The Tao of Leadership — *John Hieder.*

The first thing to do is stop.

We have looked at a number of strategies for preventing burnout or catching it before it reaches its peak. What can be done if it feels too late for that? — if you have reached the bottom of your reserves and you are very vulnerable or in crisis, emotionally and physically?

The first and obvious suggestion is: just stop! Take extended time off, quit, whatever it takes... Obvious it may be, but it can be hard to do, for so-called "practical" reasons such as "I haven't finished yet", "I need the money", "I gotta do this" etc... etc.

Merely slowing down or making little reforms is not enough at this point.

Stopping offers a chance to recuperate. It also gives much insight into just how gripping and persuasive the internal compulsions have been. Emotions that have been suppressed by all the busyness are likely to surface. Doing nothing could feel more like a struggle than a relief. The greater the degree to which our self-identity was bound up in performing the role, the greater the profound disorientation and feeling of a dissolving self-identity when we no longer have it. However, when the jigsaw of our lives is so scrambled, there is a great potential for reassembling ourselves into greater wholeness.

We may be left with unresolved feelings of guilt, failure, bitterness or disillusionment. Counseling and/or some support group involvement is very appropriate at this point. Understanding the syndrome called burnout could relieve the intensely personal involvement in these feelings and allows one to sift more carefully through the particular dynamics of our own circumstances.

SIFTING
THROUGH
THE ASHES

Some questions need to be asked:

What has been my personal contribution to this experience of being overwhelmed through work?

What factors were situational and could not realistically be influenced by me?

Was I measuring success by the wrong standards?

What are all the areas I can give myself credit for? Be very specific, write a list.

What lessons can I learn about how to live and work in a more balanced way?

What will I do differently in future?

If your physical health was significantly affected, a period of rebuilding will be necessary. At the very least a full blown experience of burnout is likely to have caused adrenal exhaustion and left your immune system compromised. But every part of the body is affected eventually by stress. You may have been "flogging the dead horse along" with stimulants such as lots of caffeine (or worse), which exacerbates the drain on the adrenal and immune systems. Good sleeping patterns, a healthy diet, relaxing time and minimal stress are needed to build these up again. It can take many months. Having a thorough check-up from a holistic health practitioner may be useful.

John A Sanford in *Ministry Burnout* makes some good suggestions for renewing psychic energy, with particular emphasis on spiritual dimensions. These reflect his Jungian outlook. He says: "The exhausted ego finds new life not through repose and rest but through a life of different and renewed activity, whether this be expressed inwardly or outwardly. It is not rest that restores, except temporarily, but tapping into energies within us that we have not yet used."[1]

We can tap new energies in several ways:

A change of outer activity.

Pursuing creative relationships to provide new inspiration and nourishment. Seek out teachers and mentors. Make a point of making some new friends, or renew old friendships by spending some quality time with them.

Using the body creatively especially if you have been sedentary. Movement that incorporates deep breathing will be most helpful, for instance: exploring drama, creative dance, singing, Tai Chi or bioenergetics.

Meditation helps with unwinding and can also cultivate insight.

Noticing dreams and fantasies. The unconscious is full of energy, and continually provides us with information on what is needed for wholeness.

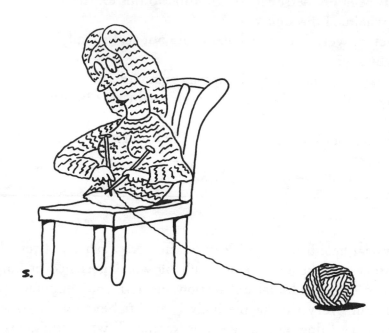

"It is not rest that restores, except temporarily, but tapping into energies within us that we have not yet used." — *John Sanford.*

Taking up new creative activities that have been very likely neglected. Did you have a hobby or craft that you used to love to do? Or is there one you have been putting off taking up? Do you have special soul-nourishing places you could revisit?

Finding ways to feed the "inner child" — by doing things like playing "kids," games, or going on explorations — remember what it's like to climb a tree or look for sea shells? These sorts of activities can tap into a deep well of energy for renewal. Let your self be a kid for a while. Find a four-year-old for tutoring!

Giving priority to self-nurturing activities will help rebuild self esteem; eg. take yourself out to lunch, make some nice things for your room, get a massage.

Creative use of comedy and parody help pry off the grip of obsession and weight of responsibility. What a relief to be irreverent about things we have been so terribly precious about! Laughter is still the best medicine.

When we have sprawled over our internal trip-wires of fatigue and self doubt, we can take the time on the ground to look for the clues. What's the trip-wire attached to? Following the wire leads us to our internal knots. Now we can either sprint off to fall again, or take the time to unravel them. Our journey after a while can then proceed further and more lightly.

EXERCISES

When we are burnt out or stressed, we often don't let ourselves have sources of nourishment or really experience them; instead we filter out the joy by staying in a negative mind set. We also cut off the direct experiencing of them by *thinking* constantly rather than stopping to *feel*. The purpose of this exercise is to reverse this trend and have a tool for nourishing yourself by simply using your imagination. I learned this exercise from Julie Henderson, a somatic psychotherapist. It can be done alone or in small groups.

Letting Yourself "Have"

Relax your whole body into a very comfortable position. Bring to mind things that really give you pleasure or nourishment. Now open your eyes and list them on paper. If you're doing this in a small group, one person acts as scribe as people say them out loud. Most importantly, pause after each one (perhaps close your eyes again) to let yourself vividly imagine that thing and to feel the sensations associated with it. Let yourself have it.

Take it very slowly and sensually. Continue for 10–15 minutes or until satiated. It might be walking on dewy grass in the morning with bare feet, sitting by a campfire, eating mangoes, having your hair stroked slowly and lovingly . . .

Now that you know how to do this, you can give yourself this remembering anywhere — sitting on public transport, before you get out of bed in the morning or when you are feeling empty.

How many of these pleasurable activities that you remembered could you arrange for yourself in the next few weeks?

The purpose of this exercise is to highlight the assets and liabilities of complaining as a stress management tool. It is, after all, one of the most commonly used ones! It also helps us let go and learn to laugh at what we have created for ourselves.

This exercise works best in pairs.

The Catastrophe Game

First individually think about all the difficult and stressful things that are active in your life currently.

Now one partner starts "catastrophizing" by choosing some of these difficulties and describing in the first person what is happening and the awful feelings involved. Thoroughly overdramatize the scene. Play the complete victim.

When the first person has finished the other partner starts in and tries to top the story with a "YOU think that is bad, well..." or something similar. The first person then gets another turn and so on. Keep it building backwards and forwards for 10–15 minutes.

At the end the partners can take a few minutes to share how in the midst of this they can take better care of themselves. Variations on this theme could be "The things I go through to save the world", "My most awful day at work" etc.

A Personal "Goodies" File

The purpose of this exercise is to compile a resource to refer to in times of high stress or discouragement, when you may lose sight of or undermine your positive qualities, abilities and talents.

Collect good references to yourself, certificates, clippings, warm letters, posters of things you have organized, affirmation sheets (see exercise p 87) or pictures of times when you felt really good. Paste them in a scrap book or place them in folders with clear plastic pages. You could also place a few of them on a notice board where you will catch sight of them. Change these regularly.

Another variation is to compile a list of all the things you felt good about in the last 6–12 months. Make a poster out of it.

Body Drawing

The purpose of this mainly non-verbal exercise is to draw attention to the needs of our physical bodies that may be neglected in the busy rush and stress of daily living. This exercise may increase motivation for applying techniques of rebalancing and healing.

You can do this exercise on your own or within a group context. You will need a roll of butchers paper or sheets of inexpensive paper as big as your body (the unused side of old posters stuck together may be suitable) and large marking pens or crayons of different colors.

1. Begin by lying down on the sheet of paper and either lightly trace the outline of your body yourself or, preferably, have someone else do it. As this is likely to be a bit sketchy, spend a few minutes fixing it up and drawing in your features such as eyes, nose, toes, to make the image more lifelike.

2. Sitting near your drawing, close your eyes and relax. Focus your internal awareness on your body and how it feels. You may need to move a little to find out where you are stiff or sore. Do a thorough internal scan with

your attention on all the parts of your body. Notice the sensations. Where is there tension? Discomfort? Where is it hard to feel anything?

3. Open your eyes and draw on your body image what you became aware of, for instance: tight shoulders, slight headache, lower back tension. Also add any other feelings and perceptions you may have about your body, eg. overweight, not very fit — but don't be too savage! You may add statements a particular body part might say if it could speak; for instance, your shoulders might say: "I've got lots of burdens" or your feet: "She doesn't even notice I'm here."

4. Now go through the body parts that were not feeling good and jot down some suggestions or draw symbols nearby about what you may need to do to bring that part back into balance, eg. tight shoulders could do with a rub, some stretching, less responsibility, and regular relaxation practice.

5. Then broaden your thinking to include the whole of your physical being. Think about it as if it were either a much loved friend or a child whom you wished the best for.

- What is this body needing for its well-being?
- What would you like to give this body in the next 12 months?
- What practical and concrete steps are you prepared to take in the next few weeks to make this possible?

---

6. Share your drawing with a partner. Take a few minutes each to share a summary of what you became aware of and what you are commiting yourself to do about it.

NOTES
1. John Sanford, *Ministry Burnout*, Paulist Press, New York/Ramsey, 1982.

Practical Help

CHAPTER FOURTEEN
Suggestions for Using the Exercises

The wide range of exercises throughout this book have been used by myself and others in all kinds of settings. Some of them are revamped old favorites that have been circulating in different contexts (I apologize for not being able to credit all the sources). Some are new. Some of them are quite suitable for individual use; others will only work as group exercises. Some exercises are valuable to introduce into meetings and other sorts of gatherings, where there is also a business agenda. Others work best in the context of a longer workshop or training session, because they require the group to feel comfortable with each other and be open to participation.

As you read the chapter, set aside some distraction-free time to work through the exercises and checklists. Consider keeping a notebook or journal to record your responses and continue the dialogue on the issues that the exercises raise for you. You may like to share these responses with someone at a later time.

USING THE EXERCISES ON YOUR OWN

If you are considering introducing a few exercises into already formed action groups, sometimes some members may feel a little suspicious or cynical about personal sharing activities. It will help if you can put the exercise in the context of a current issue for group members, either personally or politically. For instance, this could be the need to conserve energy for the long haul and the high rates of drop-outs from your group, or the need to work together more effectively on a particular campaign. Give an outline of each exercise's purpose and what will be involved.

Before you start the exercise make sure people know each other and are open to participation. (See the suggestions in Chapter 7 on inviting participation.) Do some sort of check-in before you do the other exercises (see p 89 & 109). Be careful to select appropriate exercises for your

USING THE EXERCISES IN WORK GROUPS AND MEETINGS

An atmosphere of trust is not automatically present just because people work together.

particular group. To work well, some exercises require an atmosphere of trust, which is not automatically present just because people work together or are concerned about the same issue. Encourage an atmosphere of respect, support and common ground in facing the difficult issues of these times. This will assist people to feel safe enough to express feelings and open up more about issues of concern.

TAKE IT IN STAGES
Start with a few short, non-threatening exercises that do not require much self revelation, such as the evaluation of meetings, attentive listening or creating an empowerment collage.

If they go down well, it then may be appropriate to move on to more challenging ones, such as recognizing our double lives, getting to know your rebel, the working together rating scale or the web chart for identifying stressors.

Be prepared to be flexible and adapt the exercises to suit the needs of the situation as they become apparent. Respect people's right to remain silent if they wish.

The exercises won't suit everyone; it is rare to find ones that are powerful and useful for every member of a group. Some people have trouble visualizing, for instance, while others go to sleep in relaxation exercises. Some don't like to answer a lot of questions and get more out of non-verbal exercises. If you want to lead these exercises in groups and are not sure of your ground, rehearse them in support groups or practice them with friends.

USING THE EXERCISES TO CREATE WORKSHOPS AND RETREATS

These exercises have formed the backbone of workshops and retreats lasting from a few hours to week-long programs.

Workshops have centered around such themes as:
"Despair To Empowerment — Taking Heart in Transition Times"
"Spark Without Incinerating — Nourishing Sustainable Activism"
"Where Do I Start? — Growing Into A Greener Life"
"Empowerment for Social Action"
"Team Building — Working Well Together"
"Heart Politics".

In the renewal retreat format, the schedule is much less intensive, with time between group sharing exercises for silence, meditation practice, personal reflection and creative activities. We use residential facilities with a restful, natural environment.

Workshops, training sessions and retreats have been run with already existing groups such as Environment Centers, Neighborhood Centers, youth workers and government welfare departments; also for people who gathered specifically because they were interested in exploring these themes.

FACILITATION AND GROUP LEADING

The role of the facilitator is to provide some clarity and direction while encouraging an atmosphere of safety and mutual support. A good facilitator has the ability to give attention on several levels: on the content of the discussion and on the process of the group dynamics. This means the facilitator is conscious of the needs of individuals as well as the whole group, and her/his own feelings and responses.

Many of these exercises are reasonably straightforward and do not require advanced facilitation skills to lead them. Others — such as "Telling Our Waking-Up Stories", "Finding Your Determination" or "Critic Shrinking" — require some familiarity and ease in dealing with emotions. Make sure you have done work with your own feelings of powerlessness, despair or anger about planetary or social issues first, so you are not coping with your own feelings when you need to keep your attention on the group. This does not mean clamping down on feelings — it can be very helpful and encouraging for you as the leader to share your personal feelings and experiences with the group.

If in your workshop you intend to concentrate on exercises which tap planetary concerns, I strongly recommend you first read Joanna Macy's *Despair and Personal Power in The Nuclear Age*". It is also recommended that you lead these more intensive workshops with a co-facilitator. Being part of an ongoing support or accountability group for preparation and debriefing is also very beneficial.

Other exercises may bring to the surface tensions and conflict within groups so it is important you have some group commitment to work these through. You also need to have confidence in dealing with conflict situations to guide participants towards a satisfactory resolution.

It is important to have some group commitment to work through tensions and conflicts.

Be prepared to intervene if sharing becomes long-winded or turns into a dry academic debate. Act to prevent participants from moralizing or putting each other down.

CHOOSING EXERCISES

When planning the flow of the exercises, start by thinking in terms of overall phases. The general phases I find work well are:

1. *Warming up*
   Getting to know and trust each other.
   Getting clear on people's needs, the purpose of the workshop and what you are offering.
2. *Developing* the major theme or themes.
   (Majority of the time available)
3. *Practical application*
   Setting goals, making plans for follow-up and action.
4. *Rounding off.* Dealing with any unfinished business and unresolved feelings or conflicts.
5. *Evaluation*
6. *Closing* with something positive and unifying.

Provide variety and balance in the flow of the exercises.

Provide variety and balance in the flow of the exercises. For instance verbal ones followed by more non-verbal ones, active then more sedentary ones, more intense ones followed by some lighter activities — perhaps some games, songs or relaxation. Design the workshop flexibly so you can follow where the real interests in the group are. Or be prepared to drop your program to continue an important discussion or bring a process to completion. These exercises often stimulate a lot of personal and group issues. Give people enough time to integrate them. Remember: overloading people is directly working against the purpose of the workshop!

It is always a good principle to do some evaluation at the end (See Evaluation Exercises p 101). Also be watchful for people who may need some extra support. If strong feelings are still current at the closing time, arrange some support with extra talking time, a check-in with a friend or a link with a support group. It is irresponsible to stir things up and then leave people hanging. Most times all that is needed is some empathic listening.

Have fun with these exercises and enjoy adapting them and designing your own. There is so much to explore and to share with each other on how to express our social responsibility and how to flourish while *in the tiger's mouth.*

Suggested Reading

Inner Resources for Social Change

Albert, David, *People Power — Applying Nonviolence Theory*, New Society Publishers, Philadelphia, 1985.

Chogyam, Trungpa, *Shambala — The Sacred Path of the Warrior*, Shambala, Boston & London, 1988.

Glendinning, Chellis, *Waking Up in the Nuclear Age — A Book of Nuclear Therapy*, Beech Tree Books, William Morrow, New York, 1987.

Heider, John, *The Tao of Leadership*, Humanics Publishing Group, P.O. Box 7447, Atlanta, Georgia, USA, 1985.

Macy, Joanna, *Despair and Personal Power in the Nuclear Age*, New Society Publishers, Philadelphia, 1983.

Metzger, Deena, "Personal Disarmament: Negotiating with the Inner Government", *Revision Magazine*, USA, Vol. 12, No. 4, Spring, 1990.

Moyer, Bill, *The Practical Strategist*, July, 1990, & *The Map Training Manual*, Oct., 1990, Social Movement Empowerment Project, San Francisco, CA.

Peavey, Fran (with Myra Levy & Charles Varon), *Heart Politics*, New Society Publishers, Philadelphia, 1986.

Ram Dass & Gorman, Paul, *How Can I Help?*, Alfred A. Knopf, Inc., New York, 1986.

Rubenfeld, Frank, *The Peace Manual — A Guide to Personal—Political Integration*, Lion-Lamb Press, Berkeley, California, 1986.

Seed, John; Macy, Joanna; Fleming, Pat; Naess, Arne, *Thinking Like a Mountain — Towards a Council of all Beings*, New Society Publishers, Philadelphia, USA, 1988.

Spretnak, Charlene, *The Spiritual Dimension of Green Politics*, Bear & Co, Santa Fe, New Mexico, USA, 1986.

Thaker, Vimila, *Spirituality and Social Action — A Wholistic Approach*, Vimila Programs, California, 1984.

Titmuss, Christopher, *Spirit for Change — Voices of Hope for a World in Crisis*, Green Print, The Merlin Press, London, 1989.

Walsh, Roger, *Staying Alive — The Psychology of Human Survival*, New Science Library, Shambala Books, Boston, 1984.

Communication Skills and Conflict Resolution

Bolton, Robert, *People Skills — How to Assert Yourself, Listen to Others, and Resolve Conflicts*, Simon & Schuster, Australia, 1987.

Coover, Virginia et al., *Resource Manual for a Living Revolution*, New Society Publishers, Philadelphia, 1978.

Cornelius, Helen and Faire, Shoshana, *Everyone Can Win — How to Resolve Conflict*, Simon & Schuster, Australia, 1989.

Crum, Thomas, *The Magic of Conflict*, Touchstone Books, Simon & Schuster Inc., New York, 1988.

Fisher, Roger & Ury, William, *Getting to Yes — Negotiating Agreement Without Giving In*, Business Books, Centary Hutchinson, London, 1982.

Jelfs, Martin, (revised by Sandy Merritt), *Manual for Action*, Action Resources Group, London, 1982.

Schindler, Craig & Lapid, Gary, *The Great Turning — Personal Peace, Global Victory*, Bear & Co, Santa Fe, New Mexico, 1989.

Wollman, Neil, ed., *Working for Peace — A Handbook of Practical Psychology and other Tools*, Impact Publishers, San Luis Obispo, California, 1985.

Giving Presentations

Macy, Joanna, *Despair and Personal Power in the Nuclear Age*, New Society Publishers, Philadelphia, 1983.

Milo, Frank, *How to Get Your Point Across in 30 Seconds or Less*, Corgi Books, UK, 1986.

Wollman, Neil, ed., *Working for Peace — A Handbook of Practical Psychology and Other Tools*, Impact Publishers, San Luis Obispo, California, 1985.

Working Together/Decision Making/Leadership

Avery, M. et al., *Building United Judgement: A Handbook for Consensus Decision Making*, Center for Conflict Resolution, Maddison, Wisconsin, USA, 1981.

Center for Confict Resolution *A Manual For Group Facilitators*, New Society Publishers, USA.

Coover, Virginia et al., *Resource Manual For a Living Revolution*, New Society Publishers, Philadelphia, 1978.

Doyle, Michael & Straus, David, *How to Make Meetings Work — The New Interaction Method*, Jove Books, New York, 1982.

Flood, Annie & Lawrence, Annee (Editors), *The Community Action Book* 2nd ed. NCOSS Sydney, Australia, 1987.

Jelfs, Martin (revised by Sandy Merritt), *Manual for Action*, Action Resources Group, London, 1982.

Kokopeli, Bruce & Lakey, George, *Leadership for Change — Towards A Feminist Model*, New Society Publishers, Philadelphia.

Lakey, George & Kokopeli, Bruce *Off Their Backs... and on our own Two Feet* (Overcoming Masculine Oppression in Mixed Groups), New Society Publishers, Philadelphia, USA, 1983.

Scott, Gavin; Holland, Geoff; a'Beckett, Pat, *How to Stop the Bomb — Action Handbook for Australia*, Hale & Iremonger, Sydney, Australia, 1986.

Wollman, Neil, ed., *Working for Peace — A Handbook of Practical Psychology and Other Tools*, Impact Publishers, San Luis Obispo, California, 1985.

Burnout Prevention

Sarah Conn, Tova Green, Nancy Moorehead, Anne Slepial and Peter Woodrow, *Keeping Us Going — A Manual on Support Groups for Social Change Activists*, Interhelp USA and Movement for a New Society.

Jaffe, Dennis & Scott, Cynthia, *From Burnout to Balance — A Workbook for Peak Performance and Self Renewal*, McGraw-Hill, New York, 1984.

Maslach, Christina *Burnout, — The Cost of Caring*, Prentice Hall, New Jersey, 1982.

Ram Dass & Jorman Paul, *How Can I Help?* Alfred A. Knopf, New York, 1986.

Ryan, Regina & Travis, John, *Wellness Workbook — Creating Vibrant Health, Alternatives to Illness & Burnout*, Ten Speed Press, Berkeley, USA, 1981.

Rating Scale — How Well Does Your Group Empower Its Members?

1. *VALUING INDIVIDUALS* Are positive feelings expressed and encouragement given to members?

|⌞_____⌞_____⌞_____⌞_____⌞|

Nothing positive expressed   High degree of positive feedback.

2. *CLARIFYING THE TASKS* How clear is it what needs to be done and by whom?

|⌞_____⌞_____⌞_____⌞_____⌞|

Very vague and confusing.   Very clear.

3. *EXPRESSION OF FEELINGS* How safe would you feel generally expressing feelings directly, either about the issue or about people in the group?

|⌞_____⌞_____⌞_____⌞_____⌞|

No support, very unsafe.   Strong support & safety.

4. *LISTENING & CONSULTATION* Are people consulted about things which affect them? Are they listened to?

|⌞_____⌞_____⌞_____⌞_____⌞|

No consultation, poor listening.   Consulted and listened to.

5. *RESPECT FOR DIVERSITY* Are different perspectives eg. age, ethnic, cultural, class respected and included?

|⌞_____⌞_____⌞_____⌞_____⌞|

No respect for diversity.   High degree of diversity integrated.

6. *AWARENESS OF OPPRESSION* In general is there awareness of issues of sexism, ageism, racism?

|⌞_____⌞_____⌞_____⌞_____⌞|

No awareness.   High degree of awareness.

7. *COMMITMENT TO CONFLICT RESOLUTION* Are conflicts acknowledged and resolved?

|⌞_____⌞_____⌞_____⌞_____⌞|

Conflict handled ineffectively.   Conflict handled effectively.

8. *TRAINING* Is attention given to training and skill development?

|⌞_____⌞_____⌞_____⌞_____⌞|

No attention.   High quality opportunities.

9. *VISIONING* Does your group create visions together?

|⌞_____⌞_____⌞_____⌞_____⌞|

No sharing.   Often share & encourage.

10. *FUN & HUMOR* Overall does your group have fun together?

|⌞_____⌞_____⌞_____⌞_____⌞|

Very serious, fun discouraged.   Lots of permission for fun & humor.

Index of Exercises

Index

New Society Publishers

N ew Society Publishers is a not-for-profit, worker-controlled publishing house. We are proud to be the only publishing house in the United States committed to fundamental social change through nonviolent action.

We are connected to a growing worldwide network of peace, feminist, religious, environmental, and human rights activists, of which we are an active part. We are proud to offer powerful nonviolent alternatives to the harsh and violent industrial and social systems in which we all participate. And we deeply appreciate that so many of you continue to look to us for resources in these challenging and promising times.

New Society Publishers is a project of the New Society Educational Foundation and the Catalyst Education Society. We are not the subsidiary of any transnational corporation; we are not beholden to any other organization; and we have neither stockholders nor owners in any traditional business sense. We hold this publishing house in trust for you, our readers and supporters, and we appreciate your contributions and feedback.

New Society Publishers
4527 Springfield Avenue
Philadelphia, Pennsylvania
19143

New Society Publishers
P.O. Box 189
Gabriola Island, British Columbia
V0R 1X0